The
ORAL HISTORY WORKSHOP

"*To be a person is to have a story to tell.*"

—Isak Dinesen

The

ORAL HISTORY WORKSHOP

*Collect and Celebrate
the Life Stories of
Your Family and Friends*

by CYNTHIA HART
with LISA SAMSON

WORKMAN PUBLISHING • NEW YORK

For all those whose stories will be told

Library of Congress Cataloging-in-Publication Data is available.

ISBN 978-0-7611-5197-5

Workman books are available at special discounts when purchased in bulk for premiums and sales promotions as well as for fund-raising or educational use. Special editions of book excerpts can also be created to specification. For details, contact the Special Sales Director at the address below.

Workman Publishing Company, Inc.
225 Varick Street
New York, NY 10014-4381
www.workman.com

Printed in the United States of America
First printing October 2009
10 9 8 7 6 5 4 3 2 1

Contents

Introduction

Once upon a time, a book like *The Oral History Workshop* wouldn't have been necessary. Once upon a time, when most people lived in small, tight-knit communities, with or within a stone's throw of their families. When stories, lore, and family history were essential parts of everyday life. When people spun yarns around the dinner table. When neighbors watched out for and knew everything there was to know about one another.

Nowadays, people move around for work, for better climates, for real estate deals, for fresh opportunities. Odds are pretty good that you don't know much about where your neighbors come from—and maybe you don't know that much about where *you* come from either. In this modern mobile context, it makes sense that gene-alogy is such a popular pursuit. People are starved for information about their roots; they pay to have their DNA decoded and spend time worrying about their "identities."

But there is a more direct way, a way to mine the rich sources of information all around us—just ask.

Everyone has a story to tell. And every individual is a piece of a greater puzzle—a family, a community, the wider world. This book will enable you to explore those puzzle pieces, and perhaps to come a step closer to fitting them into place.

Of course, we're talking about people here, not puzzles. About sitting down with a loved one and asking the questions you've always wanted to ask—and a great many you haven't thought of before. About capturing stories you've heard time and time again—or stumbling onto stories you've never been told. The listening process may bring you closer to those you care about, and will doubtless provide answers to questions you've had for years: "My father sold insurance for a living, but he always hinted that he'd wanted to be a doctor. He never explained why he abandoned his dream." "Elizabeth loves to tell stories about the wild times she spent traveling with her great aunt, but I've never known why she wasn't closer to her parents." "I'd love to hear our eighty-five-year-old neighbor talk about what life was like in the 1930s."

Genealogy and Your Interview

A passion for many, genealogy is the study of familial and ancestral history. Even if it's not a particular interest of yours, you're probably familiar with the basic concept of a family tree. At its core, the quest for lineage answers the question all humans (especially four-year-olds) have been asking since time immemorial: "Where did I come from?"

For many budding genealogists, the Internet has provided a veritable trove of answers. A simple search of family names can open a portal that leads from link to link to link—where all kinds of information might be revealed, from records of citizenship, marriage, and employment to the names of the ports at which your ancestors disembarked. At the end, satisfied searchers may leap up from their computers in the throes of spirited "Aha!" moments—"I found us on the Mayflower!" "Our name is in the history books!" or simply, "I wouldn't be here were it not for all of this." But the nature of the pursuit itself can be isolating; and the results, though gratifying and sometimes impressive, can seem abstract.

Personal history interviews go beyond the family tree, revealing what the ships' passenger lists, census data, and marriage certificates cannot: how your great-aunt felt as she scrimped and saved to emigrate to America, what kept her going during the times of struggle, what shaped her decisions. And they enhance and complement that family tree as well, sometimes removing untold degrees of separation between the branches: A person's memories about his grandparents or even great-grandparents will put you in touch with events that span centuries. Now that's an "Aha!" moment.

What Is Oral History?

"Oral history" refers to the practice of soliciting and recording spoken stories—stories that sometimes amount to richly detailed and emotional accounts of individual lives.

Of course, technically, oral history has been around for a long, long time. Spoken word has always been a means by which people have passed along knowledge—within families, within tribes, within religions, within neighborhoods. But both the term and the professional practice evolved in response to traditional, *written* history, a field which had tended toward a hierarchical view of things. Even if your aim is to grasp the big picture, you can't fully understand the actions of a Napoleon without also knowing what life was like for his soldiers; and those men probably didn't have biographers, nor were their stories told in the pages of newspapers—hence the need for a method that would help gather information about previously under-recorded groups.

Nowadays, the two approaches intermingle: Historians use oral histories to complement and contextualize what they glean from written documents like data-rich (but emotionally neutral) official records. Oral history gives voice to the data.

"Oral history" may or may not accurately describe what you do when you sit down to do your interview. Your interest may be casual or personal; but, like photography, oral history is a tool that can be used to create anything from casual snapshots to epic masterpieces.

Why We Wrote This Book

Cynthia's Story: On January 5, 2007, at 8:31 in the morning, my telephone rang. I remember the exact time because the ringing abruptly yanked me into consciousness, and as I lunged for the handset I saw the numbers glowing red on my digital alarm clock. I croaked a groggy "Hello?" A warm but unfamiliar voice said, "Hello, Cynthia, this is Brian Berg. I'm sorry to call so early, but I wanted to let you know that my mother passed away last night." Brian's mother, my dear, dear friend Jean Berg, had died suddenly of a heart attack while sitting at home in her favorite chair; her husband, Howard, had used CPR, called 911, and done everything he could to save her.

Two days later, on January 7, 2007, at 2:15 in the afternoon, the phone rang again. No one answered my "Hello," and after a few moments I heard a hang-up click. I found out later that it was my son, Thomas, who couldn't bear to tell me that his father had just died. Harumi had been ill for several years, but none of us had known how sick he really was. After an unexpected seventeen-day hospital stay, he was—suddenly—gone.

Jean Berg

I had had frequent and lengthy conversations with both Jean and Harumi, and if I'd thought about it (which I didn't), I would

Sure, a picture is worth a thousand words—but sometimes I wish I had a few more words to accompany the photographs in my family's collection. Take the caption my paternal grandmother, Nellie Hart, wrote on the back of this photo: "Theo, Herbert, me, Dad & Harold . . . Easter Sunday at the dinner table, 1946." The "new bride," my mother, is on the left, her eyes demurely cast down. She sits slightly apart.

Was she uncomfortable that day? Was my father's family truly welcoming?

The dish at the center of the table is decorated with a bow. Who brought it?

Where was the photo taken—in what house, town, state?

Some of my questions can be answered with a little research—but for the rest, I guess I'll never know.

—C.H.

Harumi Ando

have assumed we had lots more time to talk. Sometimes, I still find it hard to believe that they aren't around and there's no "next time"—and it's so, so sad. I knew them well—but I wish I knew more. I especially regret not asking about Harumi's childhood years, and how Jean had discovered her passions for antiques and dollhouses.

The only *good* thing about this sad chain of events is that because of the love and admiration I had for these two people, and my combined shock and sadness about their deaths, I decided to write this book.

Lisa's Story: Like most people, I love a good story. I grew up in a storytelling home where my father, Lyle Samson, was the unchallenged star raconteur. Whether it was his German grandfather's "Great Mississippi Catfish Story" or the World War II tale of his late night encounter with Chico the Gum-Chewing Wallaby, a comic touch unfailingly predominated. We loved hearing his stories and laughing over them (yes, again and again and again). Occasionally one of us would think to record Dad, and I'm so grateful to have those tapes.

You never know what kind of far-ranging application such an artifact might have. Recently, my sister Cindi and I were able to give a copy of Dad's Great Catfish recording to our cousin John Samson, the last male Samson in Ste. Genevieve, Missouri—where the tale was set. John showed us the cemetery where the first Samsons who came over from Germany were buried and took us to the county courthouse to see their land, marriage, and naturalization records. Our exchange (a recording for a guided tour) was a great example of how family history can be shared.

When I began to work in documentary film production, I was initially thrilled to stand alongside crew members as we witnessed—and recorded—the stories of a rich variety of people. In the completed films, however, these stories invariably appeared in a much shortened form.

My mother, Lois W. Samson (third from left above), was a storyteller too. Here's an excerpt from her oral memoir, which she called *Threads of a Tapestry*: "I was working in the U.S. Cadet Nurse Corps when, in the fall of 1944, there came a bolt out of the blue: a letter from my boyfriend telling me he would no longer write to me and, if he ever got out of New Guinea, that he never expected to return to our hometown.

"I was devastated, partly because all during the war I had not gone out with anyone, waiting for him to return. Instead of moping, though, I placed his picture facedown on my closet shelf and took his last advice to me, to 'go out and have fun'—which I proceeded to do with a vengeance! There was a USO where all the soldiers from the Air Force base hung out. When they had dances I would go there with other nurses and meet guys, though we had more fun when we dined and danced at the night-clubs in town. One night I wasn't in by curfew, and our redheaded captain pounced when I signed in, restricting me to quarters for a week!"—L.S.

One experience was different: an interview I conducted with a survivor of the sinking of the USS *Indianapolis*. The ratio of story recorded to story included in the final cut was familiar. The difference came from the presence of an unexpected audience: The veteran had brought his son and granddaughter along so they could hear the entire harrowing story firsthand. In all his years as a parent and grandparent, he had never fully described his ordeal to his family.

Up until that moment, I had experienced interviews as just one piece of the documentary filmmaking process. That day I learned that an interview could be an emotional catalyst, helping people overcome reticence and allowing them to share parts of themselves they might have kept hidden.

When I decided to move away from documentary film production toward a new career as an archivist—a profession that might one day help me salvage and preserve interview portions from what's known as the "cutting room floor"—I went after a master's

Lyle Samson

degree in history and archival management. My love of storytelling led me to an oral history course, through which I learned a new form of interviewing. As a fledgling oral historian, I was trained *not* to go after the ten-second sound bites that would succinctly tell a documentary's story; instead, I was to record a narrator's life story in its entirety.

These days, it's rare that we even sit still long enough to ask one another the simple questions—What did you do today? What did you have for lunch? How was your commute?—much less to thoroughly *listen* to the answers. Make the time. Gather the stories. You'll be glad you did.

The

ORAL HISTORY WORKSHOP

"*The universe is made up of stories, not atoms.*"

—Muriel Rukeyser

Before You Ask

Preparing for the Interview

YOU PROBABLY ALREADY know whom you want to interview. Maybe you've thought about approaching your parents for years and put it off—if so, you're not alone. You may even know the topics or events you'd like to learn more about or the questions you'd like to ask. If not, start off by identifying your hopes for the scope of this project. Are you interested in a certain time period—your subject's childhood or experience of a unique slice of history? Are you curious about a particular area of your subject's life—a short fling with an alternate career or life path, a previous marriage? Are there specific stories you've heard time and again and want down for the record once and for all—the elaborate prank with unintended consequences, the storied courtship? Or are you in it for the big picture—a full-scale account of your subject's life?

Of course, your plan may change as you delve into the project. And that's the beauty of human interaction: You sit down for an hour-long interview about childhood experiences, and two and a half hours later you're talking about foreign languages and apricot pie.

Better Listening with Your Third Ear

You can ask the most intriguing question in the world of the most fascinating person on earth—but if you don't know how to listen, odds are you'll end up missing a lot.

Fortunately, you can train yourself to listen with true compassion and curiosity, using what we'll call a "third ear." Imagine yourself as a tiny person sitting inside your own head, just behind your right ear, on an itsy-bitsy (but comfy) chair. From this vantage point, this extra ear can relax and absorb all that

Do you remember the first time you saw the ocean?

is said while the actual you conducts the interview. Your third ear will sense the implied meanings deep within the stories being told; detect emotional nuance; and focus on tone of voice, the emphasis placed on certain words and phrases, or the significance of a sigh or lengthy pause.

This focused listening will also help you direct the interview so that it flows naturally from topic to topic. Although you'll be guided by your prepared list of questions (see chapter 3), be sensitive to any direction your interviewee wants to take. Listen and improvise. If a particular question unearths an informational gold mine, don't just move on to the next question on your list—follow up with a logically related query. (Likewise, if a particular inquiry launches a long-winded aside that you don't feel is contributing to the picture, feel free to offer a diverting question—while trying to remain respectful of your interviewee's narrative.)

MATCH YOUR INTERVIEW TO YOUR GOALS

Once you have a sense of your general intentions, you're one step closer to figuring out what type of interview is right for you. Other factors to consider are the amounts of time and energy you can invest, how much you want to ask, and what you want to do with the information you hope to capture. Recorded interviews will give you more options, but they do require more effort.

Of course, any interview is worthwhile. You may just want to *hear* that one story of your mother's about how her long-lost puppy came home—that would be an unrecorded, conversational interview. Or you might commit to recording a series of interviews with your Aunt Diane, focusing on her time as a combat nurse during the Vietnam War—with the intention of contributing the recordings to a historical archives. (Yes, that's archives, singular—the spelling preferred by professional archivists in North America. See page 158 for more on how an archives may come to bear on your interview.)

There are many ways to describe the types of interviews that professionals conduct: focused, formal, informal, off the record, life history, topical, journalistic, structured, biographical, unstructured, and more. Much of this book is about "recorded interviews," the gold standard in oral history terms. Before you decide on your method, take into consideration your interviewee's situation, wishes, and temperament (along with your own

motivations, of course). Though you may know of or even invent other ways to conduct interviews, here are two basic approaches.

❖ *The unrecorded interview*—in which questions may be planned or unplanned; the interviewer may write down a few notes to help jog his memory later or *simply listen.* No audio or video recording or full written record is created. This method is easiest, and the experience can make for treasured memories; in cases where an unexpected interview opportunity arises, it might be the only option. Without a recording, however, those precious stories may be lost—unless the listener makes the effort to pass them on anecdotally or orally (the simple means by which many folktales, legends, and myths have stood the test of time).

❖ *The recorded interview*—in which a question list is prepared, the interview is recorded, and the tangible product (the audio or video recording) is safeguarded for posterity. A record of the interviewee's voice (and of his image, in the case of video) gives added meaning to his stories. The interview content may be shared—with the interviewee's permission—with family members and friends or other specific audiences; it may also be placed in a personal or family archives, an established oral history project, or an institutional archives where it will be available to researchers, historians, and other interested parties.

Look Beneath the Surface

"What was dinnertime like when you were growing up?" "Oh, well, we didn't tend to eat together much."

The initial response to a question may not contain a complete answer; it may, in fact, hide significant portions of the total picture. To dig deeper, you will have to quickly compose clarifying questions. "So, who usually made your dinner?" You might find out that your subject learned to cook at an early age because both of his parents worked—there's certainly a story there.

Watch out in particular for complaints, which may actually be expressions of frustration or fear. A sensitive follow-up question could spark a discussion of the subtle feelings behind the complaint—perhaps even revealing the real who, what, when, where, and why of the experience.

Let's say your subject responds to a question such as, "Education is a valuable tool. How did it affect your life?" with "I always hated school!" Don't just move on to the next question on your list; explore. And be specific. A question like "What did you hate so much about it?" or "When did you start feeling that way?" might open up further conversation more readily than a simple "Really?" or "How come?"

WHAT MAKES A GOOD INTERVIEWER

Interviewing is a skill, one in which the ordinary processes of asking and listening are used as tools for story collecting. It's not unrelated to normal conversation, but it does take some extra effort. Fortunately, it's like riding a bike—once you've learned how, you'll always be ready to go.

What makes a good interviewer? Let's take a page from two acknowledged masters of the form, Terry Gross of NPR's *Fresh Air* and Oprah Winfrey. Their questions are well researched and interesting—but so are those of hundreds of other media folks who don't inspire such good storytelling. The key is in their empathy, insight, and genuine curiosity. That's what moves guests to open up and share. (It helps that these hosts also seem to be truly at ease, comfortable with their guests and with the process.)

So what's the takeaway? Be human. Be curious. Be empathetic. And relax—your demeanor will help put your interviewee at ease.

SHHHH . . . TAKE A TIP FROM PSYCHOTHERAPISTS

Interviews are more one-sided than regular conversations—you ask the questions, he answers—but there's more to them than that. Your interviewee will be listening, too. Not just to the content of your questions, but also to the way you ask them. So be as thoughtful and engaged as you can, and let yourself be guided by a spirit of respect. Don't interrupt, and don't offer your opinions about his answers—even an offhand remark can imply censorship and cause an interviewee to clam up or withhold important parts of his story.

Listen with your mind wide open. Keep your follow-up questions empathic ("Was that tough for you?") rather than judgmental ("Why didn't you try harder?").

Interviewing does relate in some ways to classic psychotherapy. The psychotherapist's "listening process" involves more than words; it refers to all data taken in by the therapist (and by the patient)—silences, gestures, posture . . . The therapist is very, very careful about what she says, usually keeping her tone and diction neutral to avoid implying judgment. Some believe that the best mode of therapeutic "questioning" is silence—no bias demonstrated there—but that would be extreme for an interview.

Even in interviewing, though, some silence can be a virtue. Particularly if the interviewee is discussing something difficult, a breath of silence implies, "Tell me more, associate further, give me the links to this experience, fantasy, or anxiety."

So, though in preparing for your interview you'll likely focus on what you'll ask, don't forget about the power of a well-chosen pause.

Broad questions have a way of eliciting vague answers. Instead of "Tell me about high school," you might start with a smaller, more specific question: "Who were your best friends in high school?" A "little" question about a childhood game could reveal a big truth about a family dynamic. Aim for a combination of broad and specific questions to get the full story. Think of yourself as a detective. Listen for subtle clues and use your curiosity to ferret out as many facets of a story as possible. Strive to see the big picture, the larger context behind the answers you're given. Use your sense of empathy to figure out what was really going on. How would you have felt about cooking your own dinner at age twelve? You might ask other questions about family chores to try to find out whether your subject carried an inordinate amount of responsibility as a child. How did he feel when he visited other families and saw their mealtime rituals? Build question upon question.

Practice Asking

"Good listeners" are highly prized as friends and colleagues, but there's an art to *asking* as well. A question is a magic gizmo, a key that opens people up—you'll be amazed to discover what folks will tell you if you just ask. You can draw someone out without pushing or prying (it's very important to respect a person's privacy and boundaries), but don't be shy, either. If someone doesn't want to answer a certain question, he won't—but you'll never find out if you don't ask.

You can start honing your "asking skills" in everyday conversation. "Why?" is the simplest question of all, and it can be a very powerful one. Try using it more often in conversation with family or friends. Most people enjoy talking about themselves, so your practice subject will likely warm up to you as the answer unfolds. Stay in the moment, and listen more carefully than usual.

Instead of volunteering your own opinion, ask a question. If you hear "I really think our new senator is doing a great job," don't launch into why you agree or disagree—ask a question instead. "Why are you so enthusiastic about him?" will do if you can't think of anything more specific. Then sit back and listen. The more you practice, the more adept you'll become at thinking up spontaneous questions, and gradually the role of interviewer will become second nature.

Arranging the Interview

Obviously, a recorded interview isn't something you just spring on someone. You need to ask your subject for her permission in advance—you want an active, engaged participant who's willing to put some thought and energy into the process.

When you approach your interviewee, be prepared for reluctance, even for an outright "No." "Why would anyone care about my life?" she might ask. Perhaps she's averse to "dredging up all that old stuff." Use some gentle persuasion: Tell her it would be an honor to listen to her stories, and be sure to mention that you'd like to record them.

Encourage her to ask questions about the interview process. People tend to feel a lot more comfortable once they know what to expect. Explain that she will ultimately be in control of her interview—she'll decide which questions to answer and what happens to the recording.

Scheduling the Interview

Take your subject's preferences and habits into account when you're setting things up. If you're interviewing someone who is elderly or infirm, you might want to ask a few questions about his daily activities, meal schedules, any relevant health or medication matters, or other factors that might influence his availability for or receptiveness to the interview. The time of day can make a big difference: Some people are "larks" and some are "owls," and a person who is touchy and uncommunicative early in the morning might be much more open and talkative later in the day.

Find out whether your interviewee would prefer to do the interview at his home or somewhere else. Though you should leave the location up to him, make it clear that you'll need a comfortable, quiet place where you'll be undisturbed. His home may or may not fit the bill.

MEANINGFUL PROPS

Objects and visual aids can be a great boon to storytelling. Prior to the interview, you may want to ask your interviewee to gather a few photographs, birth records, passports, and other items to use as prompts: a family Bible, scrapbooks, old property records, awards, report cards, recipes, tickets. These and other keepsakes can supply vital information and help get the interviewee in the mood for reminiscing.

If the interviewee is a member of your family and you have access to a stash of family photo albums or other memorabilia, you might take the initiative and gather up any materials you think could inspire a story or two.

INTERVIEWING 101

Humans are like snowflakes: No two are exactly alike. Even people with very similar life experiences will have strikingly different stories to tell. Honor the subtleties or quirks in those stories (and the pace at which they're told). Some other guidelines to keep in mind:

❖ Don't rush—the interview process is something to be enjoyed, and people need time to gather their thoughts. Move too quickly and you may cut off your interviewee just as he was getting to the heart of the matter.

❖ Try to keep the focus on the interviewee and his story. Remember, it's *his* story, not yours, so no matter how good your rapport or how well you know the stories he's telling, do everything you can to keep the focus on him.

❖ If your interviewee doesn't wish to answer a particular question, don't insist. Do gently try to elicit the reason for his refusal or discomfort. Try rephrasing the question or explaining why you're asking. But remember, this isn't investigative journalism. It's all right to let some questions go unanswered.

❖ If your interviewee falls silent, let him pause for a bit as he organizes his thoughts. Cut into the silence too soon and you might be short-circuiting an important connection. And cut yourself the same slack: If you are at a loss for words from time to time, relax and just sit quietly to take stock.

❖ Don't fidget or rustle your papers, and be aware of any nervous noises generated by your interviewee. It's amazing what a recording device can pick up.

❖ Don't interrupt. Keep a pad and pencil handy to make quick notes about any new question you'd like to interject, and wait until there is a natural break in the narrative to do so.

❖ Be sensitive to occasional self-consciousness. Many people find it difficult to speak about themselves at length. Humor is an excellent way to move someone past a self-conscious moment, so use it every chance you get!

❖ Be tactful and respectful, no matter what your level of intimacy with your interviewee—whether it's your father, an acquaintance, or a distant relative. The interviewee is entrusting you with his story. Be gracious, gentle, and sensitive to any emotions that arise.

❖ Welcome familiar information when it comes up, even if you've heard it a thousand times; your goal isn't necessarily to unearth new information, but to create a portrait of your interviewee. Be worthy of trust. Don't judge— listen. The more the interviewee trusts you, the more relaxed and engaged he will be. As trust builds, your interviewee may be willing to respond to questions that went unanswered earlier in the interview.

A Sense of History (and a Life History Worksheet)

Prior to the interview, find out as much as you can about your interviewee. The more you know about her life and the times and places in which she lived, the easier it will be for you to choose good questions, ask thoughtful follow-up questions, and place answers in context.

Especially if you don't know your interviewee well, it may be helpful to do a little pre-interview session, using the Life History Worksheet on pages 170–171 to collect basic facts such as birthplace, age, and the names of family members. (You can do this by phone or in person.)

For extra preparation, beef up your knowledge by doing some research. Chicago in the 1940s? Read up on the time and place. Go to a library or search

Is there a particular place that you feel defined a relationship of yours? Do you go there still?

online to familiarize yourself with any major events in history that you think (or know) may have affected your interviewee. Consult contemporaneous magazine articles and newspaper reports for a shortcut to events of any recent era; memoirs or novels from the period (or set in the period) can also offer an overview.

Another way to broaden your sense of context: Reach out to colleagues, family members, neighbors, and friends of your interviewee. (Ask your subject's permission first.) They may provide invaluable details and "insider" facts.

Keeping an Interview on Track

It's a given (and a good thing) that an interview will meander, no matter how carefully you've planned your questions. But if the interviewee is venting old, negative feelings to no productive end or has gotten tied up in minutiae, you may feel you need to rein things in. What do you do to get the interview back on track?

First, try to determine whether the conversation really *is* off track. Say your interviewee is talking about her love of music and goes into an encyclopedic cataloguing of her favorite artists; if she works in the field or is just especially knowledgeable about it, this recitation might underscore her passion and contribute to a fuller picture of her personality. It might make sense to encourage her to show off her extensive scholarship rather than try to move away from the topic. Likewise, an interviewee might lapse into an academic-sounding discussion of political situations he encountered abroad, but ask yourself: Might this information be useful to a researcher someday?

If it's clear, however, that the tangent contributes little to your understanding of the subject and his life, you may try to respectfully redirect him. You might point out that, while you find the information interesting, you're concerned about the time. Make a note of the subject he was discussing and let him know that you'll come back to it if there's time left at the end of the session.

Emotional Reactions

The interview process can put us in touch with wonderful memories and bring laughter and tears of joy, but it can also stir up negative emotions. Be prepared for sadness, tears, and tensions, and try to ease them with gentle words, a touch, a hug—or just compassionate silence (whatever's most appropriate to your relationship with the interviewee). You may find yourself starting to cry, too, and that's only natural.

Some questions, though, may awaken troubling, painful, or traumatic memories. Be supportive, but don't attempt to take on the role of therapist if you haven't had the training—you are not equipped to help in that way. As the person responsible for bringing these memories and emotions to the surface, you do owe it to your

Who is the best travel companion you've ever had? Where did you go together?

interviewee to be extra sensitive and reassuring. Let her know that you recognize your part in the upset and that you care about her well-being.

If your interviewee is truly shaken, stop the interview and take a break or pick up at another time. Check in shortly after you leave. If her response is severe, consider reaching out to one of her close friends, family members, or a caregiver; you might also help her identify resources for professional help.

Deciding When to Stop

Whether it's an interruption or a difficult moment, there may be times during an interview when stopping or pausing seems like the right thing to do. Sometimes it is, but there are also times when it makes more sense to continue. Use your judgment, and consider the following suggestions:

❖ If something interrupts the interview—a ringing phone or the arrival of a visitor, for instance—it may be difficult to refocus without taking a break. It's usually best to stop recording and wait until the interviewee is able to give you his full attention again. In some instances, you may need to resume the interview another day.

DISCUSSING DEATH

You may balk at the notion of talking about death with your interviewee, but it's a universal subject—and, in fact, your interviewee may *want* to talk about the passing of loved ones.

You could say there are two kinds of people: those who have already lost someone dear to them and those who haven't yet. There can be a big difference in how someone sees life and death depending upon this one thing.

Before losing a loved one, talking about death may seem scary and abstract—taboo, in a sense. Once you understand what it's like to lose someone, that death affects everyone, you may feel that there's nothing wrong with talking about it.

If you want to discuss the losses an interviewee has experienced, his own mortality, or death in general, the best way to find out if he is willing to talk about it is to ask.

❖ An interviewee might ask you to stop recording so he can say something "off the record." Rather than stopping (which entails fiddling with your equipment and may interrupt the flow of the interview), propose skipping the question and moving on. Make a note of the dropped question and promise to return to it later.

❖ If a question triggers a long pause or brings on tears or anger, you may feel you should stop recording. Try not to, and just go with the flow instead. Stop, and you may make an interviewee feel he's being criticized or censored.

How to Handle Secrets

A special intimacy often develops between interviewer and inter-viewee, a bond that can sometimes alter the interviewee's normal sense of privacy; he may divulge personal information he had previously kept to himself.

Secrets are tricky things, and their revelation can trigger two kinds of issues, one emotional, the other legal. When you are told a secret, the implication is that you will keep it to yourself—but if you intend to share the interview in some way, that poses a problem. Help clarify your interviewee's intentions: Ask him if he *still* feels the content should be kept secret; if so, find out *from whom* and *for how long* he would like it with-held. This sort of discussion will make it easier for you to handle future access to the information.

Some secrets are benign, espe-cially when they're revealed forty or fifty years after the fact (sneaking out through the bedroom window at age fifteen, for instance). The sharing of this sort of secret isn't going to make either of you uncomfortable—it may lead to a rich conversation about first

How good are you at keeping secrets? Have you ever been told a really important secret?

loves, an adolescent's relationship with his parents, and so forth. But there are secrets and then there are *secrets*—things like physical, psychological, or sexual trauma or abuse, or criminal acts. The chances of someone's revealing any dire secrets in a life history interview are remote, but you *might* be faced with such a situation. If you are, it's likely to involve strong feelings.

Your response will depend upon the content that's revealed and your relationship to the interviewee. The revelation may be cathartic for you both. It may make you feel uncomfortable. It may make you want to help. It bears repeating that in the case of deep emotional injuries, you are not in a position to help unless you are a trained therapist or other mental health professional (especially if your interviewee is someone you don't know well).

What were you thinking about on your way down the aisle?

Often the simple act of telling one's story to a sympathetic person will bring some relief, so it's usually helpful just to listen. (Incidentally, this is one time when you *should* ask if your interviewee wants the camera or recorder turned off.) You might ask if there's anyone with whom he can talk further about the traumatic event. Check in a short while after the interview to underscore your concern and to honor what he has chosen to share with you.

What happens if your interviewee begins to share a secret that *you're* uncomfortable hearing or recording? Remember that you, as an interviewer, have rights, too. You have no inherent obligation to record anything that causes you anxiety or distress. Speak frankly about your discomfort. Tell your narrator that you are sorry for what has happened to him, but you feel uneasy recording such

What was the best crop you ever grew? How do your fruits and vegetables compare with store-bought?

information. If he is adamant about having it recorded, you might offer to facilitate his recording of these stories on his own (see "The Self-Interview," page 33).

Beware of revelations about past criminal activity; here you venture into legal territory you're probably not qualified to assess. If your interviewee admits to secret past criminal activity or describes that of others, stop the recording and have a frank discussion of the difficult position in which his revelations may place you. Hearing and recording his statements may or may not put both of you in legal jeopardy, and only a legal professional can say whether you would be required to report the admissions or accusations to federal or state authorities. In addition, if an interviewee begins to reveal confidential information about someone else, if he begins to bad-mouth someone in a manner that might be considered defamation or slander, or if he broaches issues relating to confidentiality or privacy, your recordings must be carefully handled. To help protect yourself from a potential lawsuit, consider omitting these sections from the transcripts and copies of the recordings you make available to others. (*Note:* It is beyond this book's scope to provide advice on legal matters—a legal professional familiar with local and federal law can provide proper guidance, if needed.)

Always Use Your Head—and a Written Document—to Safeguard Your Interviews

You may not realize it, but there are legal and ethical issues underlying the creation and recording of interviews. Whether or not you choose to formalize your process has a lot to do with your intentions for the finished interview. Do you want to place it in an archives? Do you want to reproduce it and share it with members of your family? In order to keep those options open, you need legal clearance from your interviewee, in the form of a signed Usage Agreement. (A sample appears on page 173.) You should consider obtaining a signed agreement even if you *don't* think you want to share your finished interviews, as you may change your mind: You never know what interesting and sharable information might arise over the course of the process.

Asking a close family member or friend to sign a legal document for an intimate recorded interview may seem a little weird, but it's worth the potential awkwardness. A written agreement will help ensure that you and the interviewee are on the same page about how the content of the interview should be treated. (Should it be for the eyes of a church group or immediate family only? Will it be part of an oral history project? Are you using it as material for a book?) In the highly unlikely event of a legal dispute, the agreement will confirm the rights you have to use the material.

In order to legally copy, share, and even just transcribe a recorded interview, you'll need a document that grants you those

---

WHY NOW?

Our lives are far more unpredictable than the weather. The old sayings "Make hay while the sun shines!" and "Get it while you can!" certainly apply to interviewing, especially when time seems limited. If your grandmother's memory is starting to fade, this is the moment for action. Even if things don't seem particularly urgent—your favorite uncle is in town for his annual visit or your mother is in a reflective mood—*now* is always the best time to jump in and get the process started. The "golden rule" of interviewing is: *Never hesitate when you see an opportunity to conduct an interview that is important to you.*

rights, signed by the interviewee. According to current United States federal copyright law, when a person creates or cocreates *intellectual property*—such as a song, a movie or, in this case, an interview recording (see box on facing page)—the creator or creators automatically own exclusive rights to its reproduction, publication, adaptation, exhibition, or performance. This means that upon completion of an interview (the moment the recording device is turned off), you and the interviewee become the sole owners of *all rights* to the work (the interview recording) until the rights are transferred *in writing*. By law, copyright cannot be transferred orally—it can only be transferred in a *signed written document*.

How does that come to bear on your project? Let's say your grandfather's stories cast light on little-documented aspects of his hometown, and someone at the local library or historical society wants to use them as part of an exhibit. What a wonderful opportunity that would be. But organizations such as libraries, museums, and academic or church archives require written documentation that the participants in the interview recording—both interviewer and subject—agree to the use they propose. If your grandfather is able to give his consent at that time, you're all set; but if he's

What do you consider an ideal vacation? What cities, countries, or parts of the world do you want to visit one day?

no longer able to do so, there will be no easy way to show that he would have approved. The modest amounts of time and effort necessary to secure a legally sound and appropriate agreement are insignificant in relation to its long-term value to the oral historian—especially if the interviews are destined for future placement in an institutional archives.

You shouldn't feel shy about asking someone to enter into and sign a legal agreement; such documents are ubiquitous these days. Whether it's an online agreement concerning software usage or a paper contract of the sort now commonly required for cell phone plans, credit cards, or even pet adoption, most adults are familiar with the requirement to "sign off" on contracts. So don't hesitate to ask your grandfather (or anyone else you plan to interview) to read, ask questions about, and sign a usage agreement.

If your interviewee trusts your judgment and you want to make it simple, here's how: The two of you can agree that you alone will control access to the interview recording, and the usage agreement will grant you the rights to the recording (which includes the bundle of rights referred to as "copyright"). This will allow you to transfer some or all of the rights to another individual, oral history project, or archives at a later date. (The sample Usage Agreement includes instructions on how to do this.) *An important note:* In transferring these rights to you, the interviewee is

INTELLECTUAL PROPERTY

Intellectual property is a term used to refer to creations of the mind. That sounds high-toned, but it encompasses a range of abstract materials, including inventions and content. Copyright laws protect intellectual property such as books, movies, music, paintings, photographs, recordings, and software, giving the copyright holder exclusive right to control reproduction and all other uses of such works; the copyright usually applies for somewhere between fifty and a hundred years from the author's death, depending on the country where the work is created.

PUBLIC DOMAIN

When intellectual property is no longer protected under a specific owner's copyright, it falls into a category called the "public domain." Once works are in the public domain, they can be used without permission, for any purpose, and by anyone.

Works enter the public domain in various ways in various countries; in the United States, they usually do so when a copyright expires.

But one can choose to place one's work into the public domain in order to dispense with copyright issues. This choice would give you the greatest access and distribution potential. If you and your interviewee want to maximize the reach of the recordings you've created, you can do so via a legal release that renounces your copyright interests. (See page 175.)

What insights have you gained about your parents over the years?

in no way giving up his right to record his stories with other interviewers, write about or publish his stories, or record them himself.

Whatever the agreement, you must respect your interviewee's wishes and protect his stories accordingly. You are cocreator of the interview, but your interviewee has the sole right to decide how his life stories will be shared. Prior to the interview, discuss your goals: what you'd like to do with the interview and any materials created from it. Let the interviewee know that it is up to him to decide who will be allowed to hear or view the recording, how the recording and its content may be used, who will hold and protect the copyright, and how and where the interview will be preserved. Make mutual decisions about these issues. Explain that it's in everyone's best interest to discuss and reach a written agreement about them.

Discussion Points

Consider and discuss the following points with your interviewee in order to create a plan of action. Document her wishes so they can be filed along with the original recording and usage agreement.

❖ Do you hope to share with others what you record? Would that include family only, or friends as well? What about community members or researchers?

❖ In what form will you grant access to the recorded interview? Will you provide unedited copies of the audio or video content to all (or only specified) family members? Edited copies? Written transcripts?

❖ Would you like the recording to be included in an ongoing

What anniversaries have you and your partner celebrated? What advice do you have for others in committed relationships?

research project at a museum, university, or historical society? Who would have access to this recording, or to the information it contains?

❖ Do you hope to submit the recording to an oral history project or an institutional archives? If so, look into submission requirements early on. What, if any, restrictions should apply? Will the recording become available to anyone, anywhere, at any time? Will personal information—name, address, contact information—be stricken from the interview?

❖ Who will control, monitor, and maintain the copyright for the interview—the interviewer, the interviewee, or both parties? A designated family member of the interviewee (for his interests) or an attorney of his choice? What about taking steps to protect the interviewer's copyright?

❖ Where will the original recording be kept? Who will be responsible for its maintenance?

Bring a Usage Agreement that reflects your interviewee's wishes and your mutual decisions to the first recording session; have her review and sign it before or just after the interview.

"*The danger lies in forgetting what we had.*"

—Adrienne Rich

Making It Happen

Recording & Troubleshooting the Interview

To BEGIN AT the beginning: Why record your interviews? Fortunately, it's an easy enough question to answer. Let's say you make the effort to interview your late mother's closest workplace confidante. What eye-opening tales you'll hear, along with the thrillingly mundane details—what they brought for lunch, their after-hours escapades, their harmless crushes on coworkers. But without an audio or video recording or written record, you'll have no way to share this real and rounded story of your mother's life with your siblings or your children. And after a few days, *you'll* begin to forget those stories; and those gestures, pauses, winks, and giggles will start to fade too.

The potential reach of a recorded interview is inherently broader, and that's why finding the stories is only the first mission of professional oral historians—the second is to record them. When reel-to-reel audio recording devices became available after World War II, they changed everything. The new machines offered convenience, immediacy, and entirely new possibilities for the field of oral history. Now that digital voice recorders and video cameras are pocket-size (and even phones can capture sights and sounds), it's easier than ever to create long-lasting records of the life stories *you* collect.

Your Recording Method

There are three basic ways to record an interview. You can, as your interviewee speaks, handwrite or type notes to create a comprehensive summary. You can use an audio recorder to preserve the soundtrack. Or you can capture the entire experience—content, visuals, and audio—with a video camera. Each method has its benefits and drawbacks, so if you haven't already chosen one, consider the pros and cons.

Handwritten or Typed

Stenographers, court reporters, and journalists are trained to quickly and efficiently capture the essence of what they hear, whether they're using a pen and paper, a laptop, or a stenograph. But for the average person, note taking isn't instinctual.

Recording an interview by hand requires intense concentration and strenuous mental juggling: You are asking questions, listening, weighing what to write down, writing it down, and formulating follow-up questions—all at the same time. Working under such pressure can take the joy out of the experience and exhaust both participants. At the very least, it's distracting for the interviewer. And, of course, you're giving yourself only one shot to listen to the interview.

On the plus side: To a nervous interviewee, note-taking may seem less formal or intrusive than video or audio recording. And your interview will already be in text form—you won't have to transcribe it—which gives you a head start on any written projects you've planned.

If note taking is the method you truly prefer—or if it's your only option—do a practice run with someone other than your intended interviewee to see how well you handle it. Are you pleased with the results? (And can you decipher your own handwriting?) For an actual interview, schedule several short sessions rather than one long one, and allow time at the end of each session to review your notes with your interviewee and make any necessary corrections on the spot. Later on, once you've begun to develop your notes into a transcript, you may need to schedule some additional conversations to clarify any lingering questions.

Would you describe yourself as an optimist or a pessimist? An introvert or an extravert?

Audio or Video

The voice of a wise octogenarian has a texture that words alone can't match. A regional or foreign accent, word stresses, a pause, a chuckle, a sigh—these kinds of auditory information contribute immeasurable depth. If you're already adept with (or willing to learn about) audio or video recording equipment, you'll be able to create a much fuller, more detailed, and more accurate portrait of your interviewee.

Today's audio recorders are small, unobtrusive, and very easy to use; they pretty much "disappear" once the interview gets under way. Interviewees who are at first hesitant or nervous about being recorded usually relax, partly because the technology is so innocent and benign. The finished product—the recording—is accessible and fun to share.

Video, of course, is the most complete of recording methods. Add a face to that octogenarian's voice: a wink, a grin, a grimace,

Who were your first playmates? Where did you meet them, and what did you play?

a wagging finger, shrugged shoulders, a demure sidelong glance at the mention of her wedding day. There's meaning in her outfit, her posture, her grandmother's ring on her right hand, the teacup collection visible over her left shoulder . . .that's all valuable information, too.

On the down side, video recording is more technically involved, and the camera can sometimes distract both participants. Because it's usually placed front and center, it's almost impossible to ignore and may cause stage fright or self-consciousness. Fairly bright lights may be needed to enhance image quality, and these can present another visual distraction.

Equipment and Accessories

There are many different kinds of voice and video recorders out there, with a variety of special features and in a wide range of prices. Some machines are designed with professionals in mind; others are more appropriate for home use. Because technology changes constantly, today's top pick may be obsolete by next year; so while it's always a good idea to check out the newest models, it may not be worth breaking the bank for innovation's sake. Depending on your level of technical acumen, you may find an older or more streamlined recorder easier to navigate—and less expensive.

For audio recording you'll need, at a minimum, a voice recorder with an *internal* microphone. Digital models eliminate the problem of unwanted operating noise from the machine itself, and they're definitely the best choice if you want to download the recording to a computer (look for models with what's called a digital direct USB feature). A model with an input jack for an *external* microphone will allow you to choose your own microphone(s) to enhance the quality of the audio you record. (See sidebar.)

For *video* recording, look for a camera that produces good-quality images in low light; has at least one input jack for an external microphone; and uses long-lasting batteries or an AC adapter so it can be powered via an electrical outlet. The first two features are optimal, but you can get away with less. The power supply, however, is critical; you really want to have an AC adapter and/or more than enough long-lasting batteries to get you through the planned length of the interview.

A *tripod* is also critical: It provides a stable platform for the camera and frees you up to interact with the interviewee. (Why go to the trouble of filming your interview only to end up with hours of shaky images?) Today's cameras don't weigh much, so an inexpensive light-weight tripod should suffice.

Buy, Borrow, or Rent

Once you've decided on the features you want, shop around; if price is an issue, see if you can borrow or rent what you need, especially if you're planning on doing only one interview. If you hope to do a series of interviews, buying may make more sense. If you can rent better-quality equipment (such as special mics or high-end cameras) than you can afford to buy, getting your equipment from a camera store or photography rental house might be a smart option.

Some high schools, colleges, or community-access TV stations will lend cameras or recorders to students or local residents. Family members or friends might be willing to help, especially if they have an interest in the interview. You'll naturally want to take special precautions to protect rented or borrowed equipment; you might even want to add it (temporarily) to your home owner's or renter's insurance policy.

MICROPHONE, PLEASE

Do you need an external microphone? You can get away with using only the built-in microphone on your audio or video recorder, but unless you're in a very quiet room, you may end up with a less-than-ideal recording.

Your choice of external microphone type will depend on the interview conditions. Lavalier or "lapel" microphones are placed, as the name suggests, at the neckline, collar, or lapel of clothing. They pick up the wearer's voice quite well—even in the case of a soft speaker in a somewhat noisy room. A small microphone set on a table or stand or attached to the top of a camera will capture a voice more clearly than most internal mics and won't pick up much ambient sound. One option is to use a "shotgun" mic for your interviewee and a lavalier for yourself, so that your questions are clearly recorded. Unless your recorder has two mic input jacks, using two external microphones will require an extra piece of equipment called a splitter.

If you want recordings of the very highest broadcast quality (created on equipment that can cost thousands of dollars), or if handling recording equipment of any kind is too much of a technological challenge for you, locate a capable local pro to help record your interviews. Although adding another person to the mix can diminish the intimacy of the experience, it will pretty much guarantee the quality of the recording. These days, videographers who specialize in family events are available in most cities and towns; a professional recording studio might also agree to take on the task. The fees for these services are high, but for some people, they may well be worth the cost.

Get Comfortable with Your Equipment

Whatever your plans for the finished interview, a clearly audible recording is essential. For the best results, familiarize yourself with your recording device and any accessories ahead of time. Read the manual (no fun, but crucial), and play around with the device until you fully understand how it operates. Test the recorder's functions (with any member of the household who'll comply) to make sure you get all the kinks out.

If you're going to be videotaping your interview, practice setting up the tripod, and experiment by videotaping a real subject. Is poor lighting obscuring facial expressions or muddying the color palette? Portable photographer's lights can help—you'll need them if the interview-site lighting is poor. Do a couple of test runs with these, too, to ensure that things go smoothly on the interview day.

Conduct a Practice Interview

If you're a total interview novice, conducting a practice interview—a dress rehearsal of sorts—will boost your confidence for the real thing. Choose someone you're comfortable with—a close friend, partner, or sibling—who is supportive of your efforts.

Have on hand everything you'll need during your "real" interview: your questions, recording device, any accessories, supplies, and paperwork. Approach this dry run with curiosity about your practice subject, even if you know the person very well—who knows what you'll find out. Choose a variety of questions from among those you're planning to ask your "real" interviewee. You may be so pleased with the results that you decide to schedule a full-length interview with your practice person!

Even a relatively short test interview should enable you to learn from your mistakes and correct them the second time around. You'll find out which types of questions worked for you and which didn't; as you listen to or watch the practice recording, make note of any technical flubs as well.

Special Interview Situations

M ost people embarking on the interview process will want to do in-person, one-on-one sit-downs with close relatives and friends, but you may have other interviewees in mind—a friend or aunt who lives hundreds (or thousands) of miles away, or the children of all the families in your neighborhood. These call for different techniques. A telephone interview might be your only option for someone you can't visit in person, and a group interview can be an alternative (or complement) to an individual conversation. Each situation requires something different—special equipment or set-ups, and perhaps a unique approach to questions and interviewing.

The Telephone Interview

A telephone interview is a good way to gather stories from someone who lives far away or from someone whose tight schedule doesn't allow for long recording sessions. Much of the process remains the same (preparing questions, securing a usage agreement, and so on), but the equipment will differ. To record both sides of the conversation, you'll

How has your place in the birth order affected your perception of yourself?

(continued on page 32)

RECORDING 101

As you begin your interview, make it your goal to talk and record continuously for the agreed-upon length of time, stopping only for short "comfort" breaks and to change recording media. Keep your energy focused on recording your interviewee's stories and making the best possible use of your precious time together. Here are a few practical tips to get you started.

❖ Begin each recording by identifying the time, place, and names of the participants. This will serve as a journalistic "time stamp."

❖ Keep track of which questions you've asked so you don't have to flounder about trying to find your place. You might write each question on a separate note card and remove cards from the set once you've asked the question. Or check questions off a list as they're answered.

❖ Don't forget to let your interviewee know that comfort breaks are allowed. A seamless recording session is the ideal, but sitting and talking can be exhausting, and some people are too polite to say they need a couple of minutes.

❖ If you stop the recording for any reason, make a note of the pause out loud ("We stopped recording to take a break") and tick off the question you stopped on.

❖ Before you resume recording after a break, check the audio by playing back a short segment; evaluate the sound quality to catch any problems and correct them. Hear an odd noise? Try to find what's causing it—maybe the interviewee's jacket fabric is brushing the microphone and making a rustling sound—and fix it.

❖ When you do restart your recording, record a time stamp explaining that you are now resuming, again giving the interviewee's name, the time, and date. Ease back into the interview by reminding your interviewee of his last answer.

❖ Reviewing a lifetime of memories can arouse emotion; if tears come, offer your interviewee tissues and words of support. And don't be surprised if the stories affect *you*—those tissues are there for you, too, if you need them.

❖ To give audio recordings a visual context, take still photographs of your interviewee (and if possible of the two of you together) at the interview location.

❖ Each of us has a different capacity for sitting still and talking. If either of you begins to tire or lose enthusiasm for the process (fidgeting or loss of focus are two good indicators), stop recording and take a break. If a break doesn't do it, suspend the session and set another time to continue.

❖ Before you finish an interview, ask yourself, "Is there one last question I need to ask in order to achieve what I'd hoped for?" Then ask the interviewee: "Is there anything that you would like to talk about?" or "What have we *not* discussed that you feel is important for me to know about you and your life?"

If you had all the time in the world and all the money you needed, what would you do?

❖ Protect your recorded media so you don't accidentally record over an earlier session. For cassette tapes, break off the small tab on the edge of the tape enclosure; for DVCAM videotape, throw the tiny switch, located at the long edge of the tape, from "Rec" to "Save"; for digital recorders, download the recording as soon as you can.

Additional Tips for Video Recording

❖ Monitor the viewfinder from time to time. Check that your interviewee's image fills the frame nicely. Adjust the camera and tripod (or ask the interviewee to shift his position) as needed.

❖ Watch out for visual distractions in the background. Anything that's moving—from a flag to a breeze-blown curtain to cars driving by outside—will draw a viewer's eye away from the interviewee. If you can't block out or remove the distracting element, move to another location.

❖ If your interviewee's image seems to be looking too dark or too washed out, adjust your lighting.

❖ To add visual interest, vary the image you've framed, either when you're changing tapes (or other recording media) or when you take a break. Come in closer or zoom out for a wider shot.

(continued from page 29)

need a small microphone (called a telephone "pick-up" or mic) that plugs into a voice recorder with an external microphone jack. To ensure that the interview isn't interrupted by a dropped call or marred by poor reception, use a landline rather than a cell phone. If either person is using a cordless phone, the batteries should be fully charged.

Obviously, a phone interview has some shortcomings. In an in-person interview your interviewee's nonverbal responses are part of the picture, helping to contextualize answers and inspire follow-up questions. Phone conversations lack this element. You can pick up nuances in the person's tone, but there's nothing quite as immediate as seeing his eyes light up, roll heavenward, or well up with tears. It's also all too easy to multitask. Your interviewee's attention can drift away to the bills on his kitchen table, the e-mail on his computer screen, or the sound of a neighbor's conversation outside his window.

However, a telephone interview may be your only option. If that's the case, be attentive to the other party's stamina and comfort. Once you get him on the line, let him settle in and get a beverage before you begin. Let him know that you can pause if he needs to take a sip of water or stretch a little.

While you can expect to talk for an hour or more, some people will tire more quickly than that—so try to ask your most important questions first, and listen carefully for clues that it's time to start winding down. A little friendly small talk before and after the interview is appropriate and can help bridge the physical distance between the two of you. Don't forget to reassure your interviewee that you are honored to hear his stories and thank him for sharing them with you.

Interviewing the Interviewer

Don't be surprised if an interviewee asks to hear *your* stories. Although in most interviews you want to keep the focus on the interviewee, trading places can be a fun and worthwhile exercise. A nervous interviewee may feel more comfortable once she knows more about you. An eager interviewee may get so involved in the process that *she* wants a turn as interviewer. Just make sure it's clear who's doing what.

There are a number of ways to approach role-reversal, depending on the timing. If the idea is raised early on, talk through some of the following options.

❖ Will you conduct the interviews separately or at the same session?

❖ Does she want to pick her own questions, or will she use yours? If the former, give her some time with the questions in Chapter 3.

❖ Who is responsible for safeguarding the recordings?

> ### DOCUMENTING CONSENT
>
> Under United States federal law and most state laws, there is nothing illegal about recording your own telephone conversations. However, certain states require documented consent, so be sure you get your interviewee's consent on tape, just in case. Wherever you are, it's considered good practice to begin by announcing that the interview is being recorded.

The Self-Interview

If you've ever buried a time capsule, written in a diary, or collected for a scrapbook, you know the instinct for preserving the artifacts of your experience for the future. Take it to the next level by recording your own story.

The self-interview process is similar to that of a regular interview: Develop your question list, or just choose topics you want to talk about; practice with your recording equipment; and set aside some time for recording.

When you're ready, sit down in a quiet place, switch on the recorder, and start telling your stories. You can give as much or as little information as you like, sticking to the facts or telling your stories like fairy tales; it's your choice—this is *your* legacy. Let family members know that you are recording your life stories—they may be interested in listening in person!

The Multiperson Interview

Remember that part in the movie *When Harry Met Sally*? No, not the deli scene—the vignettes in which married couples tell their love stories. Those may have been character actors, but the

How far back are you able to trace your roots? Your great-grandparents? Great-great-grandparents? Further? How do you know what you know?

stories rang true—and with a little hustle, you could create such a montage.

Perhaps your parents will soon be celebrating their fiftieth wedding anniversary and you'd like to make a little video of the two of them to show at the party. You won't need Rob Reiner and a Hollywood team, but it might be a good idea to have someone operate the camera while you act as producer, director, and interviewer.

The technical challenge in interviewing more than one person at a time is to record each voice clearly. For video, a camera's internal microphone is sufficient for recording two people with clear, strong voices in a fairly quiet room; with soft-spoken people, or in a room where there's considerable background noise, use lapel mics or attach an external shotgun microphone to the camera. Test the microphones you have access to in order to find out what works best for your circumstances. Have your interviewees sit close together so you can frame them in the shot. Before you begin recording, remind them to speak clearly.

Technical issues aside, the real challenge is in managing the give-and-take of the conversation, respecting each person's feelings and making sure everyone is heard—that's where you become the film's director. If you know your interviewees well, you might be able to anticipate the dynamic. (Maybe your father always jumps in first, and your mother follows up with a correction or contradiction.) Depending on the situation, you might want to set some guidelines for interview protocol. Come up with a short, clear set of rules: who gets to answer a question first (maybe you can alternate), no interrupting, how to make corrections, and so on.

Make sure everyone stays involved in the process. Pay attention to energy levels and responsiveness, making sure that no one person dominates. Think of the old variety-show trick of spinning plates on poles—you start one going, then another, then a third, then return to the first before it loses momentum.

Interviewing a Young Person

While it's easy to grasp the value in recording the full, panoramic story of an elder who's seen many eras and had many experiences, it may seem odd to ask a child or teenager to tell the story of his life. He hasn't done much yet, so what could he have to say? Well actually, he probably has a lot to say! And think what a treasure the recording will be in the future. Can you imagine how sweet it might be for a seventy-year-old man to play a recording of his own

seven-year-old voice for his grandchildren? Or for a young woman on the cusp of adulthood to hear her mother's account of the homecoming dance she attended thirty years earlier? The words of children and teens are a gift—one that can be shared, with great joy, in a variety of ways.

In order to interview any underage person, you first need to ask his parent or guardian for permission; then, of course, you'll need to ask the child. If he wants to proceed, have the parent or guardian fill out and sign a usage agreement. Discuss your interview ideas with

Who was your favorite teacher? What did you like so much about him or her?

the child, and explain how interviews generally work. If you've done other interviews that can be shared, you might want to show or play them for him.

The interview process *will* be different with a young person. A child with an extraordinary imagination may take you to some wild and wonderful places, tenaciously resisting any discussion of his "real" life. Enjoy it! And keep attention span in mind. Sitting still for long periods can be torture for a young person, so be sure to ask any important questions at the beginning of the session—and make all questions as fun and child-friendly as you can. Rather than undertaking a wide-ranging interview, start with one aspect of his life: a recent trip, a school project, an instrument he's just started to play, a sport he's passionate about.

Adolescents develop in spurts of physical, intellectual, and emotional growth, advancing toward and retreating from impending adulthood in an erratic dance. They may present maddening challenges to a prospective interviewer. A fourteen year old who is flatly uninterested in being interviewed one month may be raring to go the next. A seventeen year old will answer some questions in a precociously grown-up way while responding to others with charming naïveté. Adolescents' interior lives are complex, confusing, and often totally unavailable for discussion with adults. You'll conduct a more successful interview by focusing on concrete experiences, likes and dislikes; just as you would with any interviewee, be attentive to topics that move him in one way or another.

Helping a Young Person Record an Interview

More and more schools are introducing the idea of oral history into the classroom, having children bring in grandparents or other important elders for live show-and-tell. Why not build on this education by asking a young person to team up with you on your interview? Young people may not be up to the challenge of managing a personal history interview, but they can certainly assist you. It's a wonderful way to share the stories of a beloved family member and to teach a child that history is alive—and human. Incidentally, turning the interview into a family activity will make it seem less

formal and may cut down on any interviewee nervousness.

Give your assistant a significant part
to play. You could have her develop a
set of questions of her own and let her
ask them during the interview. You
could also rely on her technical knowledge (it may be more developed than
yours!) to help you set up for recording;
she might even act as the cameraperson.
Encourage her to take notes; they'll
come in handy if you end up creating a
transcript. (More on that on page 133.)
In short, involve your young assistant as
much as possible.

What photograph of you best captures who
you feel you really are?

The Interview Kit: An Innovative Way to Capture an Elusive Interview

Want to interview someone who really doesn't want to be interviewed, or who lives far away but isn't a good candidate for a phone
interview? Try an untraditional method: the interview kit. All you
need is a list of questions and an audio recorder. Your interviewee
will be able to go through the questions and record answers in the
privacy of his home, at his own pace, and on his own time.

It's not ideal as an interviewing technique—you won't be able
to ask for context or clarification and you won't be able to adjust
your questions in the moment—but it just might do the trick.
Some people need to be alone in order to feel safe telling their
stories, and you may be happily surprised at the results.

If the interviewee has a computer and is fairly comfortable
with technology, send a digital recorder; include directions on
how to e-mail audio files as attachments (the perfect format for
post-interview projects). If you're sending a non-digital recording
device, be sure to include plenty of blank recording media. For an
interviewee who lives at a distance, provide self-addressed stamped
packaging so he can return the materials without fuss or expense.

Common Interviewee Anxieties

I deally, your interviewee will be excited and engaged by the process. But even if he is, he'll probably also be somewhat nervous. Know that even the most reluctant interviewee may turn into a chatterbox once things get going—remember, story-telling is a human instinct—but be prepared for some common anxieties and requests.

Questions in Advance

An anxious interviewee may ask you to send a list of questions prior to the interview. Though there's nothing wrong with discussing the process in a general way, sharing questions in advance of the inter-view often results in rehearsed answers and a narrative that seems forced and artificial. Try to convince your interviewee that he will sound more natural and spontaneous without a preview. Ask him what prompted his request and try to address his concerns; you

may be able to put his mind at ease. If he's afraid of dealing with uncomfort-able subjects, emphasize that he is not obligated to answer anything he doesn't want to; if he's concerned that you might miss something important, ask *him* to prepare a few questions to give you. Many people are concerned about their ability to express themselves, or are afraid they won't have enough to talk about, or that they won't sound "smart enough"; if that's the case, offer to send a list of general subjects you hope to discuss. Remind your interviewee that this is all about his personal memories and experiences—it's not a quiz on world history or current events.

Who has been your most important role model? What did this person teach you? What about him or her have you emulated?

In any case, your list of questions will be used as a guide for the interview, not as a checklist; so you wouldn't be able to guarantee that you'd stick to your prepared list. You need the freedom to come up with spontaneous questions in response to what you learn. If your interviewee still insists on getting questions in advance, go ahead and send them—along with words of encouragement and reassurance.

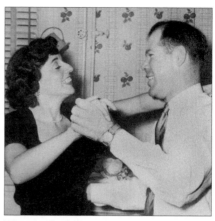

Factual Accuracy

What music makes you want to dance? What song or album will you never get tired of?

Your interviewee may worry that he won't remember or report everything accurately, that he'll misstate the facts. You can reassure him that memory is fallible, that recollections of decades past are not always accurate, and that *it doesn't matter.* Your goal is not to record the "truth"—it's to record his life story as he remembers it. If people with faulty memories were disqualified from recording their life stories, there'd be precious few oral histories in the world's archives! Let your narrator know that he'll be able to read and correct the transcript (if you intend to make one). If you are scheduled for a second interview session, you can give him the opportunity to correct previously recorded statements at that time.

Three's a Crowd

An interviewee may ask to have another person—a spouse, sibling, or adult child—present during the recording to help jog her memory or make her feel more comfortable.

Though having a third person in the room wouldn't be the end of the world, it may distract you and the interviewee or diminish the intimacy of the project. Even a silent observer can change the dynamic in a room. (And sometimes third-party chaperones are none too quiet.)

Explain to your interviewee that recording solo will help limit interruptions and give her the freedom to express herself without having to consider how her response will be interpreted by a third party. And, it will allow you to focus exclusively on her.

THIRD-PARTY PROBLEMS

Joyce, a confident, articulate woman in her eighties, was being interviewed about her life—growing up in a small Midwestern town during the Depression and then relocating to Washington, D.C., after World War II.

At one point, she became flustered because she couldn't remember the exact year she and her husband had moved East. The interviewer tried to convince her that it didn't really matter, but they ended up having to turn off the camera while Joyce went to ask her husband, Bill, to come and see if he could help her remember the facts.

The interview resumed, and soon Joyce asked Bill to fill in yet another forgotten detail. One thing led to another, and his response touched off an argument that was ultimately recorded for posterity. Not exactly the content Joyce had had in mind!

The Lesson

A third party at the interview can be helpful—or disruptive. Don't let interruptions dominate the flow of an interview. In some cases they may be inevitable, but it's your job to gently and tactfully steer the conversation back on track.

If there's no way around having a third person present—your interviewee is elderly and needs assistance or is simply too timid about the process—set the style for a smoother experience by offering the third party some information and suggestions:

❖ Stress that you're interested in the interviewee's memories—*her* understanding and interpretation of things—not necessarily the objective facts of the event.

❖ Ask the third party to hold off on making "corrections" or otherwise interrupting the flow of the interview. If he has any comments, he may jot them down and share them with the interviewee at the end of the interview.

❖ If the third party seems eager to contribute, offer to record a short interview with him once you've finished the session.

The Jitters and Breaking Conversational Ice

An interviewee who seems comfortable with the *idea* of having his stories recorded may become self-conscious when the recorder or camera is actually switched on. Making a special effort to break the ice at the outset should help anyone—from new acquaintances to your closest friends and family—loosen up.

There are several strategies for getting folks warmed up. One is to begin the session by reviewing the interviewee's Life History Worksheet or to fill it in if it hasn't already been completed. Turn on the recorder and go over it together. The simplicity of the questions should ease your interviewee's nerves.

Did you ever invent a childhood game? What were its rules, and with whom did you play it?

Other possibilities: Ask a few "icebreaker" questions (see page 51). Ask your interviewee if he has any questions for *you*, or have him explain his motivations for agreeing to the interview—what does *he* hope to get out of it? If your interviewee has assembled photographs or other memorabilia to talk about, you could start there—ask him to tell you about one of the items. With something concrete to focus on, he may relax into the experience, and you might gain insights into the best way to proceed.

Setting It Up

As the interview date draws near, make sure you've taken care of all the essentials. Call your interviewee a day or two before your first recording session and review the specifics: Confirm the date, time, and location of your meeting, and the amount of time you propose to spend together. Find out if he has anything scheduled right after the session so you can deal with potential time constraints. Offer to discuss any remaining questions he may have about the usage agreement, and remind him that you'll be bringing it along to the interview for his signature.

Equipment, Supplies, and Paperwork

The better organized you are with your equipment, supplies, and papers, the more confident and competent you'll feel. Walk in the door with everything you need in order to complete the recording, knowing for sure that you are well prepared, and you'll be able to relax and enjoy the interview. Here's a reminder of what you should bring along.

❖ Audio recorder or video camera, or pens and paper, or a computer

❖ Sufficient recording media—tapes, mini-discs, or memory card. As a safeguard, bring sufficient media to record for *double* the amount of time you have scheduled for the interview.

❖ Batteries and/or other power sources for the recording device

❖ Microphone(s), unless you are using only the recorder's internal mic

❖ Power cables, AC adapters, and microphone cables and connecters

❖ Batteries for the microphone(s)

❖ A tripod, if you are using a video camera

❖ Lights, if you've decided to use them

❖ Heavy-duty extension cords with a two-prong adapter for each cord

❖ A still camera to photograph your interviewee, especially for an interview recorded on audio. It can also be used to shoot personal documents or old photographs that your interviewee doesn't want to loan out for copying.

❖ The Life History Worksheet (page 170). If you've already filled it out with your interviewee, take it along for reference.

❖ Your list of questions. Make sure they are easily accessible and legible! Scrambled notes or sloppy handwriting can slow you down considerably or cause you to miss an important question or answer.

❖ Three copies of your Usage Agreement (see page 173).

Your On-Site Setup

By all means, arrive on time! Being prompt and well prepared shows respect for your interviewee, honors the interview process, and sets a standard for the quality of the experience. Use your first few minutes together to chat. You may be a little nervous, and he may be, too, so take this time to get more comfortable with each other. (Even a close family member may need some help warming up.)

Ask your interviewee to help you find the quietest place to make the recording; collaborating on this gets you started working as a team. Stand silently together in the room and listen: Do you hear sounds from a radiator or air-conditioning duct nearby? Is there a buzzing fluorescent fixture or ticking or chiming clock in the room? Are you close to a kitchen or laundry room? Is there a noisy group of people or a pet nearby? Avoid even slightly noise-making places if you can; disable or remove noise-making objects when possible. Interviewing someone outdoors on a sunny day may seem appealing, but check out automobile and airplane traffic, street or yard mainte-nance, and nature's own noises before settling on an outdoor spot.

If you are recording on video and aren't using lights, find a well-lighted place. Direct sun may be too glaring. Outdoors, open shade is best; indoors, strong filtered sunlight (like that coming through a sheer curtain or blinds) is ideal. A spot where you can turn on plenty of lamps and overhead lights will also work nicely. You'll have more flexibility for location choices if you are using photo lights, but those take time to set up.

If you need an electrical outlet for your equipment, look out for one when selecting your location.

PRE-INTERVIEW CHECKLIST

Before the interview takes place, you'll need to:

❖ Complete your list of questions.

❖ Organize your recording equipment, paperwork, and supplies.

❖ Address your interviewee's concerns.

❖ Agree upon the purpose and goals of the project with your interviewee.

CLOTHING GUIDELINES FOR A VIDEO INTERVIEW

Marsha agreed to be interviewed for a family history project, but it wasn't clear to her that the interview would be videotaped—so she didn't "dress up." Her casual sweater and slacks were not the clothes she would have chosen had she understood. The interview proceeded, but when Marsha watched the final edited version, she was upset: She didn't think she looked her best.

There are two lessons here: One, make sure you discuss your recording method with the interviewee in advance; two, video-recording may bring up worries about appearance. Allay anxiety by providing some guidelines: Fabric with a busy pattern, especially small repeating designs or narrow stripes, can cause a distracting vibrating effect on camera. The same goes for herringbone or houndstooth. A solid, light-colored (but not white) blouse, shirt, or jacket is ideal.

For an Audio Interview

No matter what type of audio recording equipment you're using, your set-up should address the following:

❖ Seat your interviewee in a comfortable chair.

❖ Make sure you're powered up, whether that means plugging in, precharging, or installing batteries.

❖ If possible, label the recording medium, specifying the date and the full name of the interviewee.

❖ Unless you're using a digital device, make sure you've remembered to load your recorder with the appropriate recording medium, whether that's tape, memory stick, or mini-disc.

❖ Set up any external microphones: Attach a lapel mic to the interviewee's collar, and/or set up standing mics as appropriate. Check on/off switches and batteries.

❖ Find a comfortable spot to sit near your interviewee—close enough to create a sense of conversational intimacy yet far enough away so that you both feel at ease.

❖ Perform a sound check by having the interviewee state her

name and the date, time, and location. (This will also serve as your time stamp.)

When did your family first come to this part of the world? What do you know about what life was like before then?

❖ Play back what you've recorded, evaluating the sound level and quality. You may need to experiment with the placement of your microphone, ask the interviewee to speak more clearly, or relocate to a quieter space.

For a Video Interview

The set-up for video recording is more complicated than that for audio. The good news is that if you've recorded home videos or watched others do so, you already understand the basics.

❖ Position a comfortable chair in front of a visually pleasing background—one that's not too cluttered or distracting—and have your interviewee take a seat. Locate a suitable table nearby (but out of camera range) for beverages and any other items you need to keep close at hand.

❖ Mount your camera on a tripod. Place the tripod at a comfortable distance from your interviewee—not too far away—and adjust its height so that the camera faces the interviewee head-on, looking neither down on nor up to him. (Once this step is completed, your interviewee can step away for a few moments while you finish setting up.)

❖ Power up: Double-check for batteries in your camera (or put them in now) or connect it to the power supply. If

BACKGROUND NOISE

Be attentive to any nervous habits (yours and the interviewee's) that might be picked up by the microphone. Tapping your foot, chewing gum, fidgeting in a squeaky chair, rustling papers—all will cause distracting background noise.

What are the greatest challenges or crises you have faced as an adult?

you're using electrical cords, make sure they are positioned so they won't pose a hazard to anyone walking by.

❖ Label each tape, disc, or other recording media with identifying information such as date of interview, names of interviewer and interviewee, location of interview, and the number of the recording (for example, Tape 2).

❖ Insert your recording medium (tape, memory stick, mini-disc).

❖ Have your interviewee sit in the designated spot. Set up any external microphones. (Check mic on/off switches and batteries where applicable.)

THE INTERVIEWER'S POSITION

As the interviewer, you generally wouldn't want to appear on camera except, perhaps, to provide a quick introduction at the beginning of the recording. Sit just right or left of the camera so the interviewee will be looking toward the lens when he looks in your direction.

❖ With the camera turned on but not recording, look through the viewfinder and play around with your frame. How much or how little background do you want to see? Let your interviewee's body language dictate the shot: If she sits fairly still, a tight head-and-shoulders shot is ideal. If she tends to use her hands to gesture, you'll want a wider shot—either zoom out or move your camera back.

LAST-MINUTE STUFF

Before you start the interview, make sure there are beverages on hand for both of you—talking is thirsty work! You'll also want to have a box of tissues nearby; the review of a life can stir up emotions.

Turn off all cell phones and, if possible, silence landlines.

Place cell phones some distance away from the recorder; even a cell phone in "silent" mode can generate an electrical impulse that might be recorded as audible noise. The goal of your last-minute bustling? To minimize interruptions during the interview.

❖ Perform an audiovisual check by creating a time stamp, taping the interviewee as she states her name and the date, time, and location. Play back what you've recorded, evaluating the picture and sound quality. Adjust and try again as needed. Raise or lower the tripod; move the camera; zoom in or out. All this can take some time, so ease your interviewee's nerves as you work by keeping up a bit of friendly patter.

A note on light: If the room is too bright, your camera may overcorrect by darkening the entire room. Try closing the curtains or moving away from a sunny window or bright light. If the image is too dark, find a way to get stronger light on your subject's features.

How has your relationship with your siblings evolved over time?

"A clever, imaginative, humorous request can open closed doors and closed minds."

—Percy Ross

Ask a Question, Gather a Story

Mapping Out Your Interview

I'T'S DIFFICULT TO overstate the power of a question. What you ask or don't ask has a direct influence on which stories you'll hear—and even how stories are told. If you want to know about a particular event, ask about it. (Don't wait for the topic to come up on its own—it may not.)

You may want to pursue a chronological review of your interviewee's life in order to pin down the "facts"; maybe you want the arc of his career path and personal achievements, or maybe you're interested in questions that act as windows on his inner journey—how he feels about his life experiences and what's important or truly meaningful to him. In all cases, a mix of fact-based questions and queries about emotional issues will help create a well-rounded interview.

Think about the stories you want to capture as having two layers: the broad outlines and the telling details. Sketch in a story's background by establishing a general time frame and place and by finding out what relationships and activities were central to that time and place; then paint in the color. The reasons behind a major decision, the name of a beloved dog, the tune playing in the background—those details and nuances are just as important as the events themselves.

The Questions

How to decide what to ask? No interview could ever be long enough to accommodate every interesting story a person could tell—and that inherent limitation means you'll *have* to focus on specific content. You can choose to chronicle a life path from birth to retirement, or within the confines of a marriage ("Let's start from the day you married Dad"); you can investigate a particular topic such as jobs or career development, special events, family legends, genealogy and traditions, accomplishments or personal passions; or you can concentrate on classic stories you've heard time and again.

It would take days and months, if not years, to ask all the questions in this chapter—so that approach is *not* recommended! However, you *should* read through all the questions, looking for the ones that you feel will help your interviewee tell his or her story. For each hour of interviewing, choose twelve to twenty of these questions; check off questions as you go, and type up or jot down your chosen questions in order of their importance, adding your own as needed.

Know that in all likelihood, you *will* run out of time. Unforeseen and spontaneous new questions will (and should) pop up, and you won't get all the way to the bottom of your list—which is why it's important that you begin with the questions you consider most significant.

Know, too, that those unforeseen questions may be just the tip of the iceberg. It's possible that the interviewee has his own map for the interview, his own priorities and interests, his own list of things he wants to express. You may find yourself hearing about

ICEBREAKER QUESTIONS

◆

While you don't want to leave the questions you care about most until the end of the interview (you may run out of time), you might need to get your interviewee warmed up before you dive into the meatier content. Icebreaker questions generally fall into two categories: simple, fact-finding queries ("When were you born?") and general questions on outlook ("Would you describe yourself as an introvert or an extravert?"). Use a few of the following to help calm nerves and kick things off.

When and where were you born?

What's your astrological sign?

What would you describe as the best day of your life?

When you were young, what did you want to be when you grew up?

What is your maiden name?

What nicknames have you gone by?

What foreign languages do you speak and how did you learn them?

Would you describe yourself as an introvert or an extravert? How has that affected your life?

Have you been looking forward to our interview? Why?

areas of his life that are completely unknown to you but clearly of great importance to him. Encourage him to talk about the things that matter so much to him. Don't feel that you've gone astray by setting aside your questions and exploring uncharted territory. (Of course, some interviewees will be all too happy to follow your lead—and that's fine, too.)

Without further ado, here are hundreds of questions for you to choose from. Go forth and ask!

Early Memories

◈ What stories have you been told about your birth?

◈ Where was your first home? If it wasn't your parents' first shared home, where had they lived together before?

◈ Was your birth celebrated with any cultural or religious ceremonies?

◈ What are some of your earliest memories? What images do you remember?

◈ Have you heard any stories about what kind of baby you were—easy, finicky, a screamer?

◈ When you look at your baby pictures, what family member do you think you most resemble?

Family Matters

◈ How would you describe your parents? If someone were writing their mini-biographies, what do you think would be said of them? Would you do it differently if *you* were the person doing the writing?

◈ Who would you say really raised you, or steered you through your early years? What kind of influence has that person had?

◈ Were you closer to your father or your mother? How did your feelings change or evolve over time?

◈ How would you describe the differences between your parents— their temperaments, their backgrounds, their parenting styles? In what ways did they complement each other's roles?

◈ What was the atmosphere like in your household? How did it compare with your friends' homes?

◇ Who other than your parents took care of you? Did a member of your extended family help out? A nanny or regular babysitter? How close were you to that person? What was the person like?

◇ What did your parents do for work? How do you think they felt about their jobs?

◇ What are some of your family's superstitions or quirky traditions? Where did those notions come from?

◇ What were some of the best times for your family? The toughest?

◇ Who did what chores around the house in your family? Do you think the division of duties was typical of that time period?

◇ What talents or interests did your parents bring into the life of your family? Singing, a love of nature, art?

◇ How did your parents' talents, interests, or occupations influence yours?

◇ How would you describe your parents' relationship to each other? How would you have described it as a child?

◇ Who handled money in your family? How much did you know about it as a child? Was it openly discussed?

◇ With what economic group did your family identify? Did this change as you grew up? Has your perception of your family's economic standing changed over time?

◇ How would you describe your parents' sense of style?

◇ If your mother wore a particular perfume, how would you describe its smell? How about the cologne or aftershave your dad used?

◈ What insights have you gained about your parents over the years? How do you see their lives or personalities now, as opposed to how you saw them when you were a child?

◈ What were some of your parents' favorite expressions or phrases? Do you sometimes find yourself using any of them?

◈ How happy do you think your parents were with each other? With their individual lives? What effect has their happiness or disappointment had on you?

◈ If your parents were divorced, how old were you when it happened? Do you remember what that was like? How did they tell you? What were the custody arrangements? How do you think the divorce affected you in the long run?

◈ If either of your parents remarried, what were your relationships like with your stepparents? Do you have any step- or half-siblings? What were those relationships like?

◈ If you were raised in an adoptive family, what do you know about how and why you were adopted? How much do you know about your birth parents? Have you met them? When? What was that like for you, and for your adoptive parents? How has your being adopted affected your sense of yourself? How have your feelings about it changed over time?

Siblings

◈ What do you remember about the first time you saw your younger siblings? How did you feel when they came along?

◈ How has your place in the birth order affected you? Do you think the size of your birth family has affected the size of family you want or have?

◈ If you are an only child, how do you think that has affected the way you see yourself?

◈ What do you remember of playing with your siblings? What kinds of games did you play? Indoors or out? Was rivalry involved? If so, who usually won?

◈ How did you feel about having to share things and attention with your siblings? Do you consider yourself a good sharer?

◈ What did you and your siblings argue or fight about? How did this change as you grew older?

◈ How are you and your siblings different? Similar?

◈ Do you feel that your parents compared you and your siblings? Were there unspoken comparisons? What were they about?

◈ How well do you feel you know your siblings? How well do you think they know you?

◈ How often do you see or communicate with your siblings?

◈ How did your relationship with your siblings evolve or change over time? Have you ever wished you were closer, geographically or emotionally?

◈ Have you ever envied the life of a sibling? Why?

◈ How do you and your siblings support one another as adults? To what extent do you help one another out?

◈ If you have a favorite sibling, who is it and why? Has a sibling served as a role model? How so?

◈ How do you feel the size of your family affected the amount of love, money, and space you had when you were growing up?

THE TERRIFIC TWENTY

◆

If you're looking for a shortcut, consider this list of twenty all-around great questions. Or just use these as a place to start. *Note: The questions on this list appear in no particular order. Ask them in a sequence that makes sense to you, with questions you'd most like to have answered at the top.*

Describe a typical family meal in your childhood home. What was usually on the menu? Who sat where around the table? Did it matter to you?

What do you remember as the happiest period or moment of your childhood? Who were you with and where?

What one major event shook up your life or opened up new frontiers? What memorable person, experience, or thing opened up a new world for you?

What were the best times for your family? The toughest? How did you and your family react to those?

Would you describe yourself as an optimist or a pessimist? How do you think your worldview has shaped your life choices?

If you had all the time in the world and all the money you needed, what would you do?

What is the best gift you've ever given someone? The best gift you've ever received?

Whom do you really trust? Who trusts you?

If you could take only one last trip, where would you go and with whom? What would you do?

What have you liked most about getting older? Least?

What's the biggest mistake you ever made? What did it teach you?

Who are your three closest friends? How are they different from one another, and why is each so dear to you?

Is there anything specific that you would like to talk about today?

What makes you happy? Can you pinpoint and describe some of the happiest moments of your life? The saddest?

What are the greatest challenges or crises you have faced as an adult?

What were some of your first experiences of music? What kind of music do you listen to at home? In the car? What makes you want to dance?

What health discoveries have helped you or members of your family? What discoveries do you hope will be made within the next decade?

In what type of landscape do you feel most at home, comfortable, inspired? If you could have a garden anywhere, where would it be and what would it look like? What would you grow and why?

Who or what is the love of your life?

In what ways have you managed to share your passions and interests with your friends and family?

Play

◈ What were your favorite childhood games and activities, indoors and out? Which ones have you continued to enjoy?

◈ Did you ever invent a game of your own? What were its rules?

◈ Did you have any special places to play—a fort or treehouse? How much time did you spend there?

◈ What memories do you have of favorite toys or cherished objects?

◈ What childhood games have you rediscovered as an adult? Do your children play any of the same games you played?

◈ How were dolls or action figures a part of your play scenarios? What did you do with them?

◈ What do you associate with the word *fun*? With whom do you have the most fun?

◈ How do you "play" now?

◈ Who or what always makes you laugh?

◈ How would you describe your sense of humor? What is funny to you? Are you a joke person, a pun person, an anecdote person? Do your family members share a similar sense of what's funny?

◈ How do you respond to teasing? Are you able to make fun of yourself?

◈ When was the last time you laughed so hard that your belly ached or your eyes welled up?

Elementary and Middle School

◈ What was your first school called? What kind of school was it—private, public, religious?

◈ What do you remember about your first day of school? Did you already know any of your classmates?

◈ What did you like about school? What did you not like?

◈ What do you remember about waking up on school days? How did you get to school?

◈ What did you do for lunch, and where did you eat?

◈ How did you spend recess?

◈ How did you feel about schoolwork? What were your favorite subjects? What about your report cards—what kind of grades did you get?

◈ Did you have to switch schools for middle school? What was that change like? If you didn't move to a new school, was there some kind of demarcation between elementary and middle school? And was there a difference?

◈ Describe a triumphant school moment that will always stay with you. What about a moment of disappointment or humiliation?

◈ What did you do in your free time before, during, and after school?

◈ Tell me about a middle or elementary school teacher who stands out for making a real difference in your life or is memorable in some other way. If you saw this teacher today, what would you say to them about their teaching legacy?

◈ Of all the schools you attended, which was your favorite and why? Least favorite? What was your favorite grade?

Family Vacations

◈ How did you and your family spend summer vacations? What about winter breaks?

◈ If you stayed home, were there special activities the whole family did together? If you traveled, where did you go?

◈ What was the first trip you remember? Your most memorable childhood trip? Your first time on a plane?

◈ Close to home, what were your family's favorite places to visit?

◈ If you went to summer camp, what was that like? What were some of your most memorable camp moments? Your favorite activities? How did your camp friendships compare with those closer to home?

Clubs

◈ What clubs or organizations did you belong to as a youngster?

◈ Where and how often did these groups meet, and what did you do at the meetings?

◈ If you and your friends created a club, how was it organized and what were the main activities? What rules, documents, or rituals were involved?

◈ If you created a clubhouse as a youngster, can you describe what it looked like and how it got built?

◈ How much of your childhood identity was shaped by being part of a particular club or organization?

Money and Allowance

◈ If you got an allowance as a child, did you have to do anything special to earn it? What did you like to spend your money on?

◈ Who taught you about money? What were you taught?

◈ What were your family's rules, spoken or unspoken, concerning money? Was the subject discussed openly?

◈ When you were growing up, what was your sense of your family's finances? How accurate do you think this perception was?

◈ What is the first gift you remember giving? Who taught you about gift giving, and what have you taught others about it?

Fears and Worries

◈ What was your greatest childhood fear? Where did it come from?

◈ In what situations has fear stopped you from doing something you really wanted to do?

◈ What worries or fears have you outgrown or conquered? What did the trick?

◈ What kinds of things do you worry about now? What keeps you up at night?

High School

◈ What was the name of your high school? What was it like?

◈ Which of your high school classmates did you already know from grade school? Did you keep some of the same friends? Are any of them still in your life? Which ones?

WRITING YOUR OWN QUESTIONS

◆

There are lots of reasons prewritten questions may not exactly suit the purpose of your interview. If you decide to write your own, keep in mind the classic journalist's litany: who, what, when, where, why, and how. These fundamentals are the backbone of every story (whether it's meant to be printed in a newspaper or not). As for phrasing, the following constructions are infinitely flexible: *How do you feel about* _____? *What do you remember most about* _____? *What did you think about* _____? or *Tell me about* _____.

Pay attention to the difference between "open" and "closed" questions. "Open" questions (questions that invite longer, more thoughtful answers) tend to unlock stories and let answers blossom into tales. They also help forge links between what you want to know and what your interviewee wants to tell you. "Within the family, what kind of influence did each of your siblings have?" is an example of an open question—one that allows any number of possible answers and could easily inspire a story or two. Avoid using too many "closed" questions—ones that have a yes or no answer or that will only elicit simple facts. Of course, you'll need to know the answer to questions like "Do you have siblings?" and "Where were you born?"—but try to balance those with more open-ended questions.

◈ How would you describe your level of "school spirit"?

◈ What kind of supplies and tools did you use for school? A composition book? A binder? Did you have access to a computer?

◈ Where did you hang out after school? What about on the weekends?

◈ What was your best subject? Why do you think that was? What was your worst subject? Why?

◈ What made your most boring class so dull? What about the most interesting class?

◈ Who was your favorite high school teacher? Your least favorite? Why did these teachers stand out?

◈ What high school subject or teacher led you to your career or avocation?

◈ What was your proudest high school moment? Your worst?

◈ In what extracurriculars did you participate? How heavily involved were you?

◈ Describe some of your experiences with high school dances or proms.

◈ If you graduated from high school, how did you celebrate your graduation? Who was with you?

◈ Do you try to keep in touch with any high school friends? What are they up to now? Have you gone to any reunions? What was that like?

◈ Looking back, what do you think of the education you received?

The Teen Years

◈ Describe your teenage home (or homes). What did your room look like? Did you have your own, or did you have to share?

◈ How much time did you spend at home as a teen? When you weren't home, or at school, where were you?

◈ How would you describe your adolescent relationship with your parents? With your siblings?

◈ Describe the "soundtrack" of your teen years. How often was the radio on and what was it tuned to? How loudly did you play your music?

◈ What did your parents think of your taste in music? What did you think of theirs?

◈ If you listened to music that your parents liked, what kind was it and who introduced you to it?

◈ Looking back, what do you now think of the music you listened to as a teen?

◈ What regular chores did you do around the house as a teen? Were you paid for them? How did you feel about your chores?

◈ What were your family's rules about using the telephone? Did you have your own phone as a teenager? When did you get your first cell phone?

Dating

◈ Tell me about your first date—who was it with, what did you do, and where did you go?

◈ Tell me about your first real kiss. Was it memorable? In a good way or in a bad way?

◈ What was your first "steady" relationship? How old were you? What do you remember most about it?

◈ Did you tend to "go steady" a lot? How long did your relationships last?

◈ Did you tend to go out with the same kind of person, or did you fall for different types?

◈ What kinds of gifts did you give and receive in serious relationships? What's the best gift you ever got? The worst? If you could get back one gift you gave, which would it be? Why?

◈ What's your funniest dating story? What about the bad stuff—the breakups . . . how did you handle those?

◈ People often talk about "the one that got away." Who was yours? Even if you *don't* wish things had worked out, is there one person you never really got over?

◈ What's the most romantic date you ever went on? What made it so romantic?

◈ What song defined a particular relationship for you? What about a place?

The College Years

◈ What plans did you make for yourself following high school?

◈ If college was what you wanted, what was your "dream school"? If you didn't go there, where did you go?

◈ How did your college or post–high-school experience either meet, exceed, or fall short of your expectations? How do you remember those days—as an idyll, a nightmare, something in between?

◈ What did you choose to study? What classes were required for your major or for you to complete your course of study? Did you continue learning about your favorite subjects after college?

◈ What was your first semester like? What were the challenges? The high points?

◈ What was the hardest class you took? The best? The worst? Do you remember a favorite professor?

◈ What college class, subject, or friendship opened your mind in a way that surprised you? What new worlds did it open up for you?

◈ What was your social life like? Were you in a fraternity or sorority?

◈ Do you remember your dorms or apartments? Did you have roommates? How did you get along with them?

◈ Who were your closest college friends? Are you still in touch with any of them?

◈ Did you have any wild escapades? What were they?

◈ What makes you nostalgic for your college days?

◈ Do you feel you grew up during college? If not, when did you?

◈ Have you gone to any reunions? Why or why not?

◈ If you graduated, how did you celebrate? Who came to see you graduate?

First Job and Money in the Bank

◈ What was your first job? How old were you?

◈ If you earned money while you were in high school, how did you use it?

◈ In high school and just after, how hard was it to find time for schoolwork, your job, and other activities?

◈ How did you find your first full-time job?

◈ What is the strangest way you ever found or got a job?

◈ When did you open your first bank account?

◈ Were you involved in any volunteer work early on? What kind?

◈ If you started full-time work right after high school, was it by choice or necessity? How has this decision affected your life?

◈ What was the social life like at your early jobs? What is it like for you now?

Coincidences and Luck

◈ What do you think about the concept of luck?

◈ Do you feel that you have been lucky or unlucky in general? Can you pinpoint certain instances of good (or bad) luck in your life? How often do you feel lucky?

◈ Describe a time when you feel an amazing series of events or synchronicity played an important part in your life.

◈ Do you have a lucky charm of some kind? When do you use it? Has there ever been a lucky object that seemed to work for you?

Adulthood

◈ How would you describe your transition from young adult to adulthood? Who or what helped you get through the process?

◈ Describe the moment when you realized you were truly an adult.

◈ At first, how did you feel about the independence, autonomy, and responsibility of adulthood?

◈ How do you think you measure up to your parents' achievements? Do you think that's been a factor in your life's path?

◈ Have you ever looked in the mirror and seen your mother's or father's face looking back at you? How did it make you feel?

◈ If one of your parents passed away before reaching the age you are now, how did this experience affect you as you approached the age they were when they died? And when you'd passed that milestone?

Relationships and Marriage

◈ Describe your most important romantic relationship. How did you meet? How fast did things get serious? Why do you think you chose each other?

◈ Describe your wedding day. Where was it? What did you wear? What was it like? Who were the guests?

◈ How did the relationship with your partner evolve over the years? What got better and what got worse?

◈ What do you and your partner do together for fun? Have you gone on "dates" or shared a hobby or activity?

◈ Describe the moment when your parents accepted your partner as a member of the family.

◈ How do you get along with your partner's family? Has that changed over the years?

◈ What do you think you did right in your relationship?

◈ What advice do you have for others in committed relationships?

◈ What kind of anniversaries have you and your partner celebrated?

◈ What sorts of gifts do you and your partner give each other? Which ones have been most memorable?

◈ Money can be an issue in a relationship. How have you and your partner dealt with it?

◈ What does your partner do that makes you completely blow your top? What always comforts you?

◈ What do you think is your best quality as a partner? Your worst?

◈ How does friendship come into play in your relationship with your partner?

◈ If you and your partner come from different religious backgrounds, how have you worked out which holidays to celebrate and how to mark them?

Children and Parenthood

◈ How did you feel when you first found out you were going to become a parent? Did your reaction surprise you?

◈ What were the best and worst parts of being the parent of an infant? A toddler? A youngster? A pre-teen? A teenager? A young adult?

◈ What periods of your children's growth did you most enjoy? Which ones left you most frustrated and baffled?

◈ How did you and your partner divvy up parenting responsibilities?

◈ How would you describe your parenting philosophy? How similar or different do you think it is from your parents'?

◈ How would you describe the education your children received? How did you choose the schools you sent them to?

◈ What were the main points of friction between you and your children, and how did you resolve them?

◈ What are some of your favorite things to do with your children?

◈ How did you feel when your children started dating? What can you remember of their first serious relationships?

◈ If you could go back and do it again, what would you do differently as a parent?

◈ What kinds of rules did you have in your home for your children's behavior, and how were infractions punished?

◈ What kind of trouble did your children get into?

◈ For what kinds of help or advice did your children turn to you as they got older? What rites of passage were you able to help them through?

◈ When your children went out on their own, how did you adjust?

◈ How happy do you think your children are now?

◈ How do you feel about the paths they've chosen, whether in their careers or in their personal relationships?

◈ What do you wish you'd done differently when they were growing up?

◈ In what ways do you help them? How do they help you?

Career Choices and Jobs

◈ Do you regard your work trajectory as a career, or have your jobs just been jobs? Why do you feel this way?

◈ Have you ever felt that you'd landed your dream job? Were you able to retain that feeling, or did it change?

◈ How much was income a factor in your decisions about your jobs or career? Overall, how satisfied have you been with your income?

◈ Have you ever been laid off or fired from a job? What was that like? Was the event connected to something that was happening in the larger picture—in your community or your industry? How did losing your job change you?

◈ Did you or a member of your family
ever have to move for the sake of
a job? What was the move like for
you? What about the rest of your
family?

◈ What kinds of relationships have
you had with your various bosses or
supervisors? Who was your favorite
boss, and why?

◈ If you worked directly with clients
or customers, which ones were your
favorites? Why?

◈ How much travel did your various jobs involve, and how did you
feel about this aspect of your work?

◈ To what extent did you socialize with your coworkers? If you
were inclined to maintain these relationships after you no longer
worked together, how did you do that?

Community

◈ What does the word "community" mean to you? What
community or communities would you say you belong to?

◈ In what ways do you feel connected to your community?

◈ In what civic, religious, or business organizations have you been
active? What led you to join? What did you contribute?

◈ Have you ever done any volunteer work or "given back" to your
community in some way? What motivated you? Did you find the
experience rewarding?

◈ In what special interest groups have you participated? Garden
clubs, athletic teams, book clubs, quilting circles? How did you
get interested in these groups, and how would you describe their
place in your life?

◈ Is there any volunteer work you've always wanted to do but
haven't? What do you think kept you from doing it?

◈ What have you ever done that you think might have helped the
world, in a small or large way?

◈ Have you ever helped a total stranger in a fix? What did you do?

Weekends

◈ Describe a typical weekend for you, current or past.

◈ Over the years, what have your favorite weekend activities been?
How important are those activities in the scope of your life?

◈ What do you do to recharge from
your work week? Do you have any
special rituals to help you unwind?

◈ Do you like to plan your weekends
or leave them unstructured? On
what hobbies or activities do you
spend time? How important are
these activities to you?

◈ How important have weekends been
to you in general?

◈ What kind of weekend home or regular spot have you gone to
for quick getaways? Where was it and how often did you go?

◈ What's the best weekend getaway you ever went on?

◈ Whom do you see on the weekends?

Turning Points

◈ What are the greatest challenges or crises you've faced as an
adult? How did they change your attitude toward the world
around you, or your understanding of yourself?

◈ How have you managed to cope and move on in the face of hard times? Who helped you?

◈ Describe a turning point in your life, a moment or experience that redefined your sense of self.

◈ On what or whom have you relied during rough patches in your adulthood?

◈ If you could dispense one piece of advice to someone going through a hard time, what would it be?

◈ Have you gone through periods of depression? What, if anything, did you learn from those times?

Retirement

◈ How did you know it was time to retire?

◈ How did you feel about leaving your job? Do you miss working?

◈ How was your retirement celebrated, at work or with your family or friends?

◈ What was the transition like? To whom did you turn to help you through this period?

◈ What's different about your postretirement life? Of all the things you've always imagined you'd do if you had "all the time in the world," which have you now done?

◈ How do you occupy your time?

◈ Where have you traveled since retirement? Where do you hope to go and with whom?

⬧ How do you feel about the aging process and about your current age? How has age affected your ability to do the things you've wanted to do?

⬧ What do you like most about being retired? Least?

⬧ How many of your "old" friends are still around? When do you get to see them, and what do you do together?

⬧ Have you been able to spend more time with loved ones since you stopped working? What sorts of things do you do together?

Grandchildren

⬧ Describe how you felt when you first became a grandparent. How old were you?

⬧ How has grandparenting changed you?

⬧ What do your grandchildren call you? Did you choose that name or did they?

⬧ How often do you see your grandchildren, and what are some of your favorite things to do with them?

⬧ How is grandparenting different from parenting? Have you ever taken on a parenting role with your grandchildren? Lived with them or had them come live with you? What was that like?

⬧ Most grandparents spoil their grandchildren. How do you spoil yours?

⬧ What's your favorite part of being a grandparent?

⬧ How has having grandchildren changed your relationship with your children?

Holidays, Parties, and Gifts

◈ What were the most memorable holidays of your childhood? Your lifetime? Tell me about the first one you remember.

◈ What were your favorite holiday gifts during your childhood? Your least favorite?

◈ How did you celebrate Halloween as a child? What were your favorite costumes and places to go trick-or-treating?

◈ What kinds of fireworks displays or parades do you remember?

◈ How has your experience of holidays changed over the years? What roles have you taken in the celebrations? Which holidays do you celebrate now, and what's usually on the menus?

◈ If you and your partner came from different religious backgrounds, how did you go about deciding which holidays to celebrate and how to mark them?

◈ What kind of a gift giver are you? Do you make your gifts or shop for them? Who is always on your list? What sorts of gifts do you like to receive?

◈ Describe a typical holiday meal during your childhood. Where were holidays typically celebrated, and who came over? What dishes were usually served? Who did the cooking?

◈ Describe a party you've been to—yours or someone else's—that epitomizes your idea of a great celebration. What made it great?

◈ What kinds of parties have you thrown as an adult? What are the best parties, large or small, you've hosted?

◈ What's your favorite holiday meal? Who best prepares it?

Sweet Memories

◈ What period or event can you pinpoint as the happiest time of your childhood? Who was with you, and where were you?

◈ What have been the best times of your adult life?

◈ What was the most unexpected birthday gift you ever received? The one you pined after?

◈ Describe a perfect day. Where would you go, what would you do, and who would be with you?

◈ Where and when are you happiest to be alone?

◈ How were birthdays celebrated when you were growing up?

◈ What has always been your favorite possession?

◈ What are your warmest and most cherished memories?

◈ What stands out as your most romantic moment?

Clothes

◈ What were your feelings about your clothes when you were young? How important was it to you to look like the other kids?

◈ What's the first piece of clothing you remember wearing? Loving?

◈ What special-occasion outfit do you remember from your childhood? Describe a favorite everyday outfit or specific item of clothing.

◈ Did you have any homemade clothes? What did they look like, and who made them for you?

◈ As a teenager, what fashion trend or movie icon did you admire and emulate? How would you describe your teen look? How different or similar was it from that of your peers?

◈ Over the years, what trends have you followed? Flouted? What's the most regrettable look you ever bought into?

◈ What outfit from your past makes you cringe?

◈ Have you kept any of your favorite clothes from earlier eras, and if so, where are they stored?

◈ How has your look—clothing, hairstyle, and so on—evolved over the years? Would you be able to break the changes down into phases?

◈ What's the best item of clothing you've ever had? Do you still have it? Do you still wear it?

Rites of Passage

◈ Over the course of your life, what rites of passage have been of greatest significance to you?

◈ Who taught you to ride a bike? Where did you go on your first bike? How far were you allowed to stray?

◈ How old were you when you first were allowed to stay home without a babysitter or older sibling? How about when you first stayed up until midnight on New Year's Eve? What did you do to make sure you stayed awake?

◈ When and where were you first allowed to go out on your own? What was that like?

◈ With whom did you have your first live-in relationship? How did you adjust to the experience of living together?

◈ If you had children, what changed in your life when your first child was born? How did having your subsequent children change you and your family's dynamic?

The Wider World

◈ What do you think of the times you've lived through? Have you ever wished you'd lived in a different time period? Which one? Why?

◈ What were some of the biggest news stories and world events when you were growing up? How much do you think you understood about what was happening? Did these events affect you and your family?

◈ What were the big names in the news when you were young? Which ones were you interested in?

◈ What kinds of world events were discussed at home?

◈ What innovations or inventions have most affected your life? Which one could you not imagine living without now?

◈ When did you become aware of politics and what was the catalyst?

◈ For whom did you cast your first vote?

◈ How involved did you become in the political process? How involved were other members of your family?

◈ What causes or candidates have most excited or interested you in recent years? Over the course of your life?

◈ Have your political leanings changed over time? How so?

Travel

◈ What do you consider an ideal vacation?

◈ What kinds of vacations did you and your family take together when you were young?

◈ What sorts of trips have you taken as an adult? Which were the most successful, and what made them so memorable?

◈ How often and why were you required to travel for work? Did you enjoy it? What were the rewards?

◈ Have you ever taken a vacation by yourself? What was that like?

◈ What sorts of places are you drawn to? Why do you think that is?

◈ What are some of your most vivid travel memories?

Hopes and Dreams

◈ When you were a kid, what did you want to be when you grew up? Where did you get the idea, and what about it appealed to you? Did you ever imagine you'd end up where you are now?

◈ What did you daydream or fantasize about as a child? Did you ever make up a different life or reality? What was it like?

◈ What hopes or dreams would you say you've brought to fruition? What dreams have you set aside? Any regrets?

◈ What's the silliest or most unrealistic ambition you've ever had?

◈ What's the most outlandish desire you've ever had?

◈ What is your "road not taken"?

◈ What do you still hope to accomplish?

◈ When you were in high school and college, where did you picture yourself ten or twenty years later?

◈ If you could build a dream home anywhere in the world, where would you put it? What landscape would surround it? What would the house itself look like?

Friends

◈ Who were your first playmates? Where did you meet them, and where did you play?

◈ Who was your first best friend? Name some of the "best friends" you've had over the years. What made you want to be friends with each of them?

◈ What kind of imaginary friends did you have? What were their names, and what kinds of roles did they play?

◈ If you and your friends had sleepovers, what were they like?

◈ With which of your childhood friends have you remained close? Why do you think the friendships lasted so long?

◈ Are there friends from whom you've grown apart, whom you still wonder about?

◈ How did your friends and friendships shift from childhood to high school, and from high school on?

◈ How did you make new friends once you were done with school?

◈ How do your friendships from childhood compare to those from later in life?

◈ What sorts of things do you do with your friends these days? How often do you see them?

◈ Which friend, past or present, knows you best?

◈ Which friend do you go to for help? Which friend or friends come to you?

◈ Have you had any friends who've served as role models? What did you admire about them?

◈ What's the strangest place you ever made a friend?

◈ What friends do you consider family?

◈ How important has friendship been in your life?

◈ If you are married or in a committed relationship, how would you describe the friendship you share with your partner?

Religion

◈ What was the influence of your family's religion on your life?

◈ What services did you attend? How often? How involved were you in your religious community?

◈ If you went to a religious school, how did this shape your experience of religion?

◈ What kind of coming-of-age celebration did you have as a young teen? What was it like?

◈ How were religious holidays celebrated in your home?

◈ How did your religious beliefs or level of involvement change over time? What traditions do you observe now?

◈ How were you raised to think about other religions?

◈ Did getting out in the world expose you to religions or beliefs you hadn't experienced through your family? What did you take away from these new realms?

◈ Have there been times when you've lost your faith? What do you think was the cause?

◈ Have you ever had a conversion experience? What was it like, and how did it affect your life?

◈ How do you now feel about the religion you were raised in? Do you still practice it? Why or why not?

◈ How would you describe your concept of God?

Losses

◈ Do you have any memories of how you pictured death, or what happens after a person dies, as a child? How do you picture it now?

◈ Did you experience any personal losses or spend time with anyone who was terminally ill during your childhood? What do you remember about that?

◈ What losses have you experienced in your adult life? Which ones were the hardest to live through, and how have they changed the way you live your life today?

◈ How have your feelings about death and dying changed as you've grown older?

◈ What do you miss most about family members and friends who have passed on?

◈ How do you want to be celebrated when you die?

◈ What are your beliefs about the afterlife?

◈ What memories and mementos do you cherish most from the friends and family you have lost?

Good and Bad Behavior

◈ What was considered "good" behavior in your family?

◈ What kinds of behavior were considered "bad"?

◈ What's the worst thing you did as a child? What's the worst thing you did as a teenager? Do you regret it?

◈ When you broke the rules at home, how were you disciplined? At school?

◈ Have you ever been tempted to cheat? What stopped you—or did you do it?

◈ Was there a "good" child in your family? Who was it?

◈ What sorts of things did you do that your parents didn't know about? Did you ever end up telling them? If not, why?

◈ As far as your parents were concerned, what was the worst type of offense?

◈ What was your first lie? When do you use "white lies"?

◈ Were you ever on the receiving end of pranks, practical jokes, or bullying?

◈ What's the best prank you ever pulled?

◈ Have you ever betrayed a friend? Why and how?

◈ Have you ever wanted to take revenge on someone? What did you do, and why?

◈ What's the worst thing you've ever done?

◈ When do you feel disappointed in yourself? What do you do to make things right?

◈ Have you ever been arrested? Why? Were you tried for the offense?

◈ When you were growing up, what kinds of experiences did you and your friends have with drugs and alcohol?

Secrets

◈ If you've ever kept a diary, what sorts of things did you write in it?

◈ In general, how good were you at keeping secrets as a child? If you weren't good at it, why not?

◈ Have you been told any really big secrets? Did you keep them?

◈ What were some of your family's secrets?

◈ What secrets have you kept from your family?

◈ What would most people be surprised to know about you?

Nature

◈ What is your favorite season? Can you explain why? What did your hometown look like during this season, as opposed to the place you live now?

◈ You're on your way home on a spring, summer, fall, or winter day as a child. What do you see, hear, and smell, and how does this make you feel?

◈ What is the most dramatic weather you've experienced?

◈ When and where did you first see an ocean? Snow? What was that like for you?

◈ What early experiences of nature made an impression on you?

◈ What are the most magnificent mountains you've ever been on and what did you do there?

◈ If you maintain a garden, what does it look like? What do you grow in it?

◈ Do you have any natural objects in your home—rocks, seashells, and the like? Where did you find them? Why do you think these objects appealed to you?

◈ Have you gone fishing, hunting, or bird-watching? When and with whom?

◈ Do you like taking walks or hiking? Where do you like to go?

◈ What's your favorite time of day?

◈ What is the most beautiful place you've ever seen?

The Places Called Home

◈ Tell me a little about all the places you have lived. What brought you to each new place? How long did you live in each?

◈ What town do you consider your hometown and why? What do you love about it?

◈ What was your hometown neighborhood called, and what was it like? How did it compare with other neighborhoods?

◈ How did your hometown or neighborhood change during your childhood? Over the years, or after you moved away?

◈ What were some of the places in your hometown that were important to you? What made them so? What did you do there?

◈ What do you remember about your hometown celebrations, such as fireworks displays, Memorial Day parades, annual picnics, or holiday festivities? How did you and your family participate?

◈ To what extent do you identify with your hometown?

◈ What is your earliest memory of your childhood home? What can you remember of its colors, sounds, smells?

◈ In how many homes did you and your family live over the course of your childhood? Which one stands out as a favorite?

◈ What were your childhood homes like? How did they compare to those of friends or extended family?

◈ Imagine that you're sitting in the living room of your childhood home. You get up and go to the window. What do you see?

◈ Describe one of your childhood bedrooms. What did you see through your bedroom window?

◈ Describe a favorite room in your home or a favorite outdoor space nearby.

◈ What was directly outside your home? Did you typically go outside to play?

◈ If you moved away from your hometown, what were you looking for? Did you find it? What did you miss?

◈ What do you love about the place you call home now?

Cars and Other Vehicles

◈ How old were you when you learned to drive? Who taught you?

◈ If you didn't learn, why not?

◈ What was your first "set of wheels" like? What types of cars were popular at the time?

◈ Where was your favorite place to go in your car, and who would you take along with you?

◈ What kind of importance have cars had to you over the years? How often have you changed cars?

◈ What's your favorite of all the cars you ever had? Do you still have it?

◈ What kind of a driver are you? What's the most memorable driving experience you've ever had? The worst?

◈ What kind of driver would your partner, children, or friends consider you to be?

◈ What car did you always want but never get, and why?

Sports and Outdoor Pursuits

◈ How old were you when you learned to swim? Who taught you?

◈ Where did you usually go to swim as a kid? Where did you prefer to swim—in pools, lakes, swimming holes, rivers, or the ocean?

◈ Who taught you to ride a bike? Do you remember graduating to a big-kid bike?

◈ What kind of games did kids in your neighborhood play? Did you join them?

◈ In what organized sports did you participate during grade school? High school? College? How important was that to you? Is it still?

◈ What sports were you especially good at? Any particular reason why?

◈ Who are or were your sports heroes? What sport or team do you follow? How often do you watch? What do you like so much about this particular sport or team? Do you play or wish you could?

◈ How has your game improved as you've aged? Worsened?

◈ Is there a social aspect to the sports you play or watch or to the hobbies you pursue?

◈ In what ways have your "extracurriculars" complemented your professional work? Do you see any connection? Are there any activities you've pursued largely *because* they were helpful to you in your job?

◈ What other outdoor activities do you enjoy?

Arts and Creativity

◈ In what ways was art a part of your childhood or schooling?

◈ What kind of art or music were you exposed to early on? Did you go to museums or galleries? To see music, dance, or theater? What did you see? Who typically took you on these outings?

◈ Did you make art at home? What was your first "medium"? What materials did you use as a child? What were your favorites?

◈ What was your childhood art like? Was there a particular focus? Did it reflect an imaginary world or a certain topic, for instance?

◈ If you still have any of the artwork you made as a child, who kept it for you? Is there a piece you wish you still had that's lost or missing?

◈ What sorts of things have you made as an adult? In what way is art a part of your life now?

◈ What hung on the walls or decorated the surfaces in your childhood home? What's in your home now?

Music and Dancing

◈ How were you introduced to music? What kind of music did you hear at home?

◈ What was the first song you remember hearing? Singing?

◈ If you took music lessons, where did you take them and with whom?

◈ How did you choose your first instrument? Do you still play it?

◈ If you ever played in a band or orchestra or sang in a choir, what were some of your best—or worst—early performance experiences? Did you ever perform solo?

◈ What kind of music did you listen to as a teenager? How did your tastes change as you grew up?

◈ What did your parents think of the music you listened to? Looking back, what do you think of it?

◈ What kind of music do you listen to now? Do you have an extensive music collection?

◈ What album or song will you never get tired of? What makes it so listenable?

◈ What kind of music always makes you want to dance? What kind of music have you *never* been able to dance to?

◈ What is your favorite musical era?

◈ Did you take dance or acting lessons when you were young? What kind? Did you perform?

◈ When and where do you dance now?

Health

Note: *If you want to collect more information about health or medical issues with your interviewee, check out the forms at www.familyhistory.hhs.gov.*

◈ What was your health like as a child? What do you remember about visiting the doctor or dentist?

◈ If you've had any serious illnesses or injuries, what were they and what treatment did you receive?

◈ Have you ever had to go to an emergency room or stay in a hospital? What for? What was it like? What about other members of your family?

◈ Have you ever been to see a counselor or therapist? What prompted you to seek help?

◈ What kinds of exercise programs have you followed to keep healthy? How old were you when you started exercising?

◈ How would you describe your overall health patterns?

◈ What changes have you noticed in your health or fitness as you've gotten older? How have you changed your lifestyle in response? Has your diet changed?

◈ How have your tastes in food changed over time?

Partners and Soul Mates

◈ What do you think your life would have been like without your life partner?

◈ How would your life have been different if you and your partner had met ten years earlier or ten years later?

◈ Describe how you and your partner fell in love.

◈ What was your relationship like *before* you fell in love?

◈ When did you decide to get married, and why? If you decided not to marry, what went into that decision?

◈ What was the proposal like?

◈ What was the hardest thing to get used to about living with your partner?

◈ What do you think was hardest for your partner to get used to in living with you?

◈ Have you ever been close to splitting up? Why, and how did you resolve things?

◈ How often do you spend time apart, and how important is this time to each of you?

◈ What's the longest you've ever been apart, and what was the reason for the separation? How did it affect your relationship?

◈ To what extent do you think you and your partner have come to resemble each other?

◈ How do you think your partner has changed you?

◈ If you've lost your partner, what has life been like for you since his or her death?

Food Experiences

◈ What is your first memory of food?

◈ Describe a typical family meal. Who usually cooked? Did you help? What did you eat? Who sat where?

◈ Who did the grocery shopping? Where did you go? Were any foods grown at home?

◈ Did you ever go out to eat as a family, or order food for delivery or takeout? Regularly or just on special occasions? What were your family's favorite restaurants, and what did you like to order?

◈ If any foods were grown at home, what were they? Who tended the garden?

◈ What kinds of snacks did you usually have around the house? What snacks weren't you allowed?

◈ What do you remember about your first times helping to cook?

◈ What were the first things you cooked on your own? Where did you get the recipes? For whom did you cook?

◈ How often were cakes, pies, cookies, and breads baked in your home? What kinds?

◈ What kind of birthday cake did you typically get, and what was your favorite?

◈ What foods did you love as a child? What foods did you absolutely loathe? How have your tastes changed over time?

◈ Were there certain foods you weren't allowed, or that you were allowed only as a special treat?

◈ What was usually in your school lunch? Did you take it from home, or get it from the school cafeteria?

◈ Where did you go out to eat and hang out with your friends as a teen?

◈ How have your food
   tastes evolved over time?

◈ What did you typically
   do for lunch in high
   school?

◈ Have you ever
   experienced serious
   hunger? What were the
   circumstances?

◈ What are your favorite foods now? Least favorite?

◈ What is the best meal you ever had? Who were you with?
   What do you think made it so good?

◈ Describe your ideal meal.

◈ What's the strangest food you've ever eaten? What food will you
   never, ever try?

◈ How is your cooking different from or similar to your parents'?

◈ Do you remember the first time you drank alcohol? What was
   that like?

◈ What's your favorite drink? What drink can't you tolerate?

Movies and Television

◈ Describe your family's television viewing habits when you were
   growing up. What shows did you regularly watch together?
   How did you decide what to watch as a group?

◈ What were your favorite shows when you were young?

◈ What shows do you like to watch now?

◈ What's the first movie you ever saw? Who took you? What do
   you remember about the experience?

◈ What kinds of movies did you like as a youngster? What about now?

◈ What's your favorite place to watch movies?

◈ Have you ever felt that a television program or movie changed the way you saw yourself or the world? How so?

◈ If you could live the life of any of your favorite television or movie characters, which one would you choose? Why? What would you do as that character?

◈ What are the highlights of your television and movie DVD collection? How do you decide what to purchase?

◈ What's the film you've watched the most times? How many times do you think you've seen it and what's its appeal? How do family and friends respond to your passion (or obsession)?

◈ What phrases from TV shows or movies have worked themselves into your vocabulary?

Books

◈ What are some of your favorite books? To what types of books or authors do you gravitate?

◈ What are some of your favorite books from your childhood? What did you love about them?

◈ What kinds of books have given you the most reading pleasure over the years? The greatest challenge?

◈ How often do you read, and how do you decide on a book?

◈ What does your bookshelf look like? Do you tend to keep your books? How do you decide what to keep?

A FEW OF THEIR FAVORITE THINGS

◆

Though the "favorite things" category won't necessarily give you the deepest insight, it can be used to create a fun and creative portrait of your interviewee. To generate discussion, simply say "Tell me about your favorite _____." Follow up with a simple "How come?" or "Why?" if desired. This quick and easy tactic should stimulate memories and work wonders to lighten up an interview.

Actors and actresses	Gift	People	Radio station or show	Television shows
Animals	Holiday	Pet	Restaurants or types of restaurants	Thing about yourself
Artists	Indoor activities	Photo of yourself		Thing you've made
Authors	Job	Piece of clothing	Sandwich	Time of day
Books	Magazine	Place to relax	Sayings	
Car	Movies		Scent	Toy
City	Musical group or band	Place to travel to	Season	Type of exercise
Color		Place to worship	Smell	Way to meet people
Drink	Musicians		Songs	
Family activities	Newspaper	Place you've lived	Sports teams	Way to relax
Flower	Outdoor activities	Play		Way to travel
Foods	Outside spaces	Political figures	Stage of life or age	Weekend activity
Game	Part of the newspaper	Possessions	Sweets	Year or decade
			Teachers	

◈ What book have you read over and over? How many times do you think you've read it? Has the reading experience changed over time?

◈ What books have changed the way you perceive the world, or some part of it?

◈ If you could take three favorite books with you for a long, isolated stay in a mountain cabin, which would they be?

Ancestry and Lineage

Note: *If you're interested in mapping out a detailed family history (whether it's yours or someone else's), you're going to need to do some targeted fact-finding. The questions and prompts in this category can help to give you a full, rounded sense of your subject's lineage.*

◈ Tell me about the family into which you were born. How far back are you able to trace your roots? Your great-grandparents? Your great-great-grandparents? Further? How do you know what you know?

◈ Where do the various branches of your family come from?

◈ How did your ancestors get to the country where you were born? Do you know exactly where they first settled, and the reasons for their various moves?

◈ What kind of work did your ancestors and members of your extended family do?

◈ What do you know about any legendary ancestors? Famous or infamous characters? Just plain characters? Tell some stories about them.

◈ Who acts as family historian? How does he or she share information with the family?

◈ How much do you know about your grandparents' lives? What stories have you heard about their childhoods? Their adult lives?

◈ What are the memorable stories in your family, those that are passed on and told again and again? Who told them to you, and who tells them best? What about stories that were told once and never forgotten?

◈ Have you ever been to a family reunion? How was it? Whom did you meet that you'd heard about but didn't really know? What new relationships or information emerged?

◈ What written records of your family's history have been preserved? What about keepsake documents such as passports, immigration or naturalization records, birth certificates? How far back do these go, and what is their significance to you?

◈ What are the traditional given names in your family, the names that pop up generation after generation? Is yours one of them?

◈ How do you feel about your heritage—religious, cultural, geographical, and so on? In what ways does your lifestyle deviate from your heritage? In what ways do you live it?

Family Awareness

◈ How many members of each generation of your family do you know or remember? Who are they?

◈ How many aunts and uncles do you have? Great-aunts and -uncles? What are their names? Of the ones you've known, who was your favorite?

◈ What is your earliest memory of your grandparents? Your great-grandparents?

◈ If your grandparents lived nearby, how often did you see them? What did you typically do with them? What are some of your favorite memories of them?

◈ If your grandparents lived far away, what do you remember of your visits to them and their visits to you?

◈ What were your grandparents' homes like? How were they different from yours? What were the best rooms or parts of their houses?

◈ What special things did your grandparents do with you that your parents did not?

◈ Outside of your nuclear family, were there any family members who contributed to your development in some way? What lessons did they teach you?

Life Records and Other Documents

◈ What documents do you have from your birth, such as a birth certificate, birth announcement, or baptismal certificate? Where are they kept?

◈ What photos have you seen of yourself as a baby? As a child or teen? Where are those photos now? How often do you look at them?

◈ Describe clothing, toys, or presents given to you as a baby that you cherish and still have, or that you just remember.

◈ How did your family document itself visually—in home movies, slides, or photographic prints? How and with whom were they shared? Where are these images now?

◈ What artifacts from high school and college do you still have? Your diplomas? The tassels from your mortar boards? Class rings? Yearbooks? Where are these items stored?

Special Things and Family Heirlooms

◈ What special family heirlooms do you have? Who gave them to you, and how long have you had them?

◈ What do you know about the objects' history—who held onto them before the person who gave them to you, and before that? Who owned them first?

◈ How do you use or display your heirlooms? What do they mean to you and to your family?

◈ What do you know about the person who first owned or made each of the objects in your collection? How did you find that out?

◈ What plans do you have for the future of these heirlooms?

◈ Are any of the items particularly valuable in a monetary sense? How does that influence your handling of them and your feelings about them?

For the Record

◈ What do you care about above all else? When and why did this become so important to you?

◈ What major life lessons do you feel you've learned, and how do you apply them?

◈ Would people call your basic attitude about life optimistic or pessimistic, and why do you think that is? Has this changed as you've gotten older?

◈ Who taught you to read? Who read to you before you could read yourself? Can you remember your favorite childhood books?

◈ If you could change one thing you did in the past, what would it be?

◈ What are the major world events that have directly affected your life?

◈ On a scale of 1 to 10, how would you rate your happiness during your childhood? Your adolescence and early adulthood? Your adult life?

◈ Who or what did you care about above all else as a child? As a young adult? As an adult?

◈ What is your favorite photo from childhood? High school or early adulthood? Adulthood?

◈ What photograph of you best captures who you feel you really are?

◈ Who has been your most important role model? What did this person teach you? What about them did you emulate?

◈ Who showed you the most kindness?

◈ What do you feel are the most important lessons you have ever learned? What lessons have you taught others?

◈ If you could keep just one memory in your heart for all eternity, what would that be?

◈ What wisdom about life and the world in general would you like to share?

◈ What makes you proud?

◈ How do you think your family will remember you? Your friends?

◈ What would you like your legacy to be?

◈ What have you wanted to know about *me* but have never asked?

◈ What was the angriest you've ever been? What did you do as a result of this anger? Do you wish you could change what you did?

◈ What is your greatest regret?

◈ If your house were on fire and you had time to rescue only three items, what would they be and why?

◈ What have you been willing to gamble on over the years? To what extent have these gambles brought you rewards?

◈ What haven't you done that you wish you had, and do you think you might still do it?

◈ What haven't you had enough of in your life?

◈ Describe a special moment when you were lucky to be in the right place at the right time.

◈ What was your biggest personal challenge as a child? As a teen? As an adult?

◈ How have you changed as a person since childhood?

◈ What was your biggest mistake? What did it teach you?

◈ Tell me about your current hopes, dreams, and fears for the future.

◈ Tell me about a recurring dream you've had throughout life, and what that dream has come to mean to you.

◈ What have I not asked you about yourself that you think is important for others to know?

Specialized Questions

(for Serious Gardeners, Cooks, Artists, and More . . .)

Some people develop passions and interests that define them and characterize substantial portions of their lives; some follow paths or have experiences that stand apart from the main. If you are planning to interview an artist, chef, musician, gardener, writer, actor, entrepreneur, or a member of the armed forces—or deciding on questions for an animal lover, passionate traveler, serious collector, or committed activist—you'll find questions in the following "specialty" groups that will help you delve deeper. No matter whom you're interviewing, doing your research and choosing the right questions will ultimately result in a uniquely individual portrait.

The Immigrant Experience

◈ When did you come to this country, and how old were you?

◈ Who came with you on the trip here? Who, if anyone, met you when you arrived?

◈ What country did you leave? What precipitated the move, and how did you feel about it?

◈ What are some of your fondest memories of your old home?

◈ What did you think when you first got here? What do you remember of those first few days or weeks?

◈ What did you find it difficult to adjust to? What did you love?

◈ Where did you live when you first arrived, and how did you end up there? Did you know anyone there—friends or family members? Were there other people who came from the same place you did?

◈ How long did it take for you or your parents to find work? Was it similar to what you or they had done before?

◈ How did your or your family's economic status change after your move? Was that a motivating factor?

◈ What was learning a new language like? How did you learn? Did you know any words or phrases before you moved?

◈ When do you speak your first language now? How comfortable are you in your native tongue?

◈ What are the differences between the two languages? Which do you prefer?

◈ Has life been better here than in the "old country"? Worse? In what ways? How does it compare overall?

◈ What was it like to start school in a new country? How different were schools here?

◈ Which holidays from your old country did you continue to celebrate? For how long?

◈ When did you feel you really belonged?

◈ When did you become a citizen, and what was the process like? What did it mean to you? How did you celebrate?

◈ How did you keep in touch with the people you'd left behind? Did you see them again? Why or why not?

◈ How did you try to make sure that your children stayed connected to the language and traditions? If you didn't, why not?

◈ What do you feel your children have missed by growing up in this country? Gained?

◈ How often have you been back to visit? In what ways do things over there seem different to you now?

◈ How do you think the experience of relocating has changed you?

◈ What about your homeland do you miss the most? Of the foods you grew up with, are you able to get or make some or all of them here?

◈ What about your homeland do you miss the least?

◈ Is anything still strange to you about this country? What seemed strange at first but now seems normal?

Passionate Travelers

◈ When did you first get the "travel bug" and why?

◈ What is it that you like so much about traveling?

◈ What do you remember about the first trip you took as an adult? Where did you go and with whom? What did you do?

◈ If you have ever traveled alone, where did you go? Did you like it?

◈ What cities, countries, or parts of the world have you loved, or longed, to explore?

◈ Who's the best travel companion you've ever had? What's the most amazing trip you've ever taken? The most disappointing?

◈ What type of traveler are you— a planner or a wanderer?

◈ What's the most interesting food or meal you've eaten while traveling? The best? The worst?

◈ What experience have you had of making friends while traveling? Falling in love?

◈ What sorts of souvenirs have you brought home? What one or two items do you treasure the most?

◈ What's the funniest thing that's ever happened to you on a trip?

◈ To what place would you most like to return?

◈ Have you ever wanted to jump ship and move to one of the places you visited?

◈ What's the most amazing thing or place you've seen?

◈ Prior to traveling to a new destination, what kind of study do you make of the history of the place—or do you discover it as you travel? Do you try to learn the local language and customs?

◈ How do you document your travels? Do you like to take lots of photos or write in a journal? Do you look at your travelogues often once you're home?

◈ How has travel changed your worldview?

Living Abroad

◈ If you've lived abroad, in what places did you live, and under what circumstances? How long did you live in each country?

◈ What do you remember of the cultures in which you lived?

◈ What language skills did you pick up, and how? What was the learning experience like?

◈ How did your time abroad shape you? What parts of that culture do you still hold onto? Foods? Holidays?

◈ How did you maintain your connections while you were away? Were you in touch with friends and family back home? How often did you see them?

◈ What was it like to come home?

◈ Have you gone back? Why, and what was the visit like?

◈ If you became an expatriate as an adult, why did you relocate?

◈ What challenges have you had raising your children abroad?

◈ How has moving away affected the way you think about your "passport" country?

◈ How do you think living abroad changed you or your perceptions?

Military Service

◈ If you joined the military by choice, why? What did you hope to achieve by enlisting, and how did your family respond?

◈ Which branch did you enter? What attracted you to it?

◈ If you were drafted, how did you feel about having to go into the service?

◈ When you left home, what were your good-byes like?

◈ Where did you go for basic training? What was the hardest part? What friendships do you remember from that time?

◈ What were some of the greatest challenges you encountered overall?

◈ How did your training in the military compare to your friends' experiences going to college or to work?

◈ In what military conflicts did you participate, and what were your duties? Did you see combat?

◈ What was your experience of combat? What helped you get through it? What have been the effects on you and on your family?

◈ What changes did you feel in yourself as you went through these experiences?

◈ Describe one of your most memorable homecomings.

◈ What special training did you receive during your time in the service?

◈ Did you reenlist after your first tour? Why or why not?

◈ What were the highlights of your service?

◈ How did your service affect your loved ones? Did they travel with you to your various posts? What was that like for them?

◈ Which post was your favorite? Your spouse's favorite? Your children's favorite? Why?

◈ What was the most challenging aspect of life in the military? Were you ever tempted to drop out?

◈ What is your assessment of the overall conflict in which you participated?

◈ What was military food like? Describe a typical meal. Is there anything you won't eat now because of your years in the service?

◈ Who were your friends? What did you do together when you weren't on the front lines? Have you stayed friends?

◈ What were the hardest physical challenges? How did you cope?

◈ Were you ever wounded? How did your injury happen, and how and where were you cared for afterward?

◈ Were any of your friends wounded or killed in combat? How did those losses affect you in the field? How do they affect you now?

◈ How has your military experience shaped the person you are today?

◈ When you were in other countries, how much of the culture were you able to explore?

◈ What was your R&R time like? Where did you go and what did you do?

◈ How did moving up through the ranks change things for you?

◈ Who inspired you during your service? How?

◈ How often do you talk about your wartime memories, and with whom? Was there a time when you couldn't talk about them?

◈ How has your service affected your close relationships?

◈ Looking back, was the military the right choice for you?

◈ Are you involved with veterans' organizations? Do you stay in touch with anyone from that time? How are these friendships different from those you made at other times?

Entrepreneurial Spirit

◈ What other jobs or careers did you have before you decided on the one you are in now? In what ways did earlier career choices lead you to this one?

◈ Did you always want to have a business of your own? What has entrepreneurship meant to you?

◈ When did you start to train for your current job or career, and what was that training process like?

◈ What person or institution was most valuable in training you? Have you ever had a mentor? How did the relationship develop? What has this person taught you?

◈ Whose business advice do you take, and why?

◈ Where did you first hang your shingle or set up shop? What did your first professional space look like?

◈ How did you finance your business?

◈ How did you choose the name of your business?

◈ What were the biggest obstacles you faced starting out? Through the years?

◈ What kinds of competition have you faced? Has competition been a motivator to you? What did you do to make your business stand out?

◈ To what professional organizations do you belong? How have they been helpful?

◈ What have been the most difficult financial problems your business has faced? How did you resolve them?

◈ Have you ever come close to closing up shop? Why?

◈ How long did you run the business alone before hiring help? Who were your first employees? Your best and worst hires?

◈ Who are your business role models or heroes? How have they inspired you?

◈ To what extent has work blended into your personal life? What would you say that's been like for your family?

◈ Are you able to take pride in your professional accomplishments? How do you measure your professional growth?

◈ When did you feel that your business was going to be okay? When did you feel success was in your grasp?

◈ What were your proudest moments in your work life?

◈ What special relationships have you developed with clients, coworkers, or employees over the years?

◈ What plans do you have for the future of your business?

◈ What do you think you would have done to make a living if you hadn't done what you did?

◈ Where do you think your work ethic comes from?

◈ What have you loved most about your work? Least? In what elements do you think you excel, and where do you think your weaknesses are?

◈ If you inherited or took over a family business, how had you been groomed for it? How did family members pitch in to help you? How did that work out, and how did it change your family dynamic?

◈ What plans do you have for the future of your business?

Dedicated Athletes and Sports Fans

◈ When did you decide you wanted to become an athlete?

◈ What have been some of your greatest personal athletic triumphs? Your worst defeats?

◈ Who are your sports heroes? Have you ever seen them play live?

◈ Which sports did you play as a child? How big a part of your life were they?

◈ Why do you think you ended up playing the sport you play?

◈ What do you do to keep in shape?

◈ When you close your eyes and remember being on the field or in the arena or on the court before a competition or a game, what sights, sounds, smells, textures, and tastes do you recall?

◈ What's your first memory of watching or listening to a professional sports game? Where were you, and who was with you?

◈ Who taught you the rules of the game? How interested were you in the intricacies of scoring?

◈ Which sports do you follow? If you only follow one sport, why? Do you or did you play it?

◈ Who took you to your first real game? What teams were playing?

◈ How big were sports in the town where you grew up? How often did you go to games?

◈ Have you stayed loyal to your hometown team?

◈ How has your love of sport affected your choices in life—the college you went to, the town you moved to, the places you vacation?

◈ What's the farthest you've ever traveled to see a game? Why was it so important to you?

◈ Who shares your passion? How?

◈ Does your partner share your passion for the game? If not, has that created difficulties?

◈ How has watching professional sports affected your game?

◈ What player or players do you identify with? Why? Which of them did you get to meet, and where did you meet them?

◈ What kind of sports memorabilia do you collect, and where do you display it?

◈ How do you feel when you watch sports? How do you act? How do you react when your beloved team loses?

Animal Lovers

◈ Did you grow up having pets? Which ones were your favorites?

◈ How did your family or you decide when to get a new pet, and where did you get them?

◈ How old were you when you got your first pet? What kind of animal was it and where did you get it? Who named it? Can you remember how excited you were?

◈ Name as many of your pets as you can remember, from when you were a child until now. Describe their personalities.

◈ Who took care of family pets? What was involved in their care, and what were your responsibilities?

◈ Did you ever have several pets at the same time? When, and what were they? Did you ever keep a whole litter of kittens or puppies?

◈ Where and how did you play with your pet? Did your pets sleep in your room, or in bed with you? Did they have their own beds?

◈ How long did your pets live? What was your first experience with a pet's death? What kind of burial or ceremony did you have for it?

◈ What are your favorite kinds of pets?

◈ How have you participated in rescuing animals or helping pets in need? What experience have you had taking in a stray animal and keeping it as a pet?

◈ What's the most unusual pet you've ever had and why did you choose it? Where did you get it?

◈ When did you first get a pet in your own household and what was it? How did you train it?

◈ What role have pets played in your adult life? Do you keep pets for companionship, to protect your home, or for some other reason?

◈ What's your favorite kind of animal? What is it that you love so much about it?

◈ Tell me about your experiences with horses. Where and how did you learn to ride? If you ever owned a horse, where did you stable it and how often did you ride? If you only "rented" horses, where did you do this?

◈ What horse gave you the most exciting ride? Where were you?

◈ If you grew up on a farm or ranch, which of the animals did you love or loathe caring for?

◈ How do you think human and animal companionship differ?

◈ What animals have you traveled long distances to see? Why did you want to do this?

◈ What experiences have you had with marine animals? Whale watching? Diving with stingrays?

◈ If you are a bird-watcher, what are the most exciting experiences you've had birding? What's the rarest specimen you've seen? What species are you excited to see feeding at your bird feeder?

Food Lovers and Cooks

◈ What were your favorites among the dishes you grew up with? Do you make these now? From memory or from a recipe?

◈ In your childhood home, where did food tend to come from? A market? A garden?

◈ Describe special meals that were shared with extended family and friends when you were growing up. Who was there? What were the occasions that brought you together? What did you do to help out?

◈ Describe a typical dinnertime with your current immediate family. In what ways is it similar to or different from what you experienced growing up?

◈ Who taught you to cook? If you taught yourself, how?

◈ What home economics or cooking classes did you take in middle school or high school? Have you taken classes at a cooking school?

◈ Which interested you more when you were young, baking or cooking? Why do you think that was, and how did your interest change as you grew up? Which do you prefer now?

◈ Where do you get your recipes? Word of mouth, cookbooks, magazines, a recipe collection? What family recipes do you have?

◈ Do you have any "secret" recipes you'd be willing to divulge now?

◈ Which cookbooks are your tried-and-true favorites?

◈ How does your cooking differ from what you grew up with? What memories do you have of what went on in the kitchen in your childhood home?

◈ What was your first kitchen like? Where did you get your dishes and cookware? Were any of the items inherited?

◈ What do you like to cook? What do you not like to cook?

◈ What are some of the most memorable meals you've cooked? For whom did you cook them and what did you make?

◈ Do you enjoy sampling unfamiliar dishes and recipes?

◈ What newfangled cooking equipment have you embraced, and
what have you rejected? Why?

◈ How involved were you in teaching your children and/or
grandchildren how to cook?

Gardeners and Their Gardens

◈ What do you think brought you to your love of flowers and
gardens? What are some of your earliest garden memories?

◈ What do you enjoy more, working in gardens or looking at them?

◈ As a child, with whom did you garden? What did you like best
about gardening with this person?

◈ What garden work was your responsibility? What did you most
like to do? What was your least favorite job? Did you have your
own little garden plot?

◈ If your garden supplied the family table with fruits and vegetables,
what kind were they? Which was your favorite and how did you
help in its planting, care, and harvesting?

◈ What plants, flowers, and trees do you love the most? Have you
grown them? What types of gardens—herb, vegetable, flower—
have you had? Which do you prefer?

◈ Where do you get your favorite plants, seedlings, cuttings, or
seeds? To whom do you pass seeds and cuttings along? Do you
consider yourself a plant collector or advanced gardener?

◈ Describe browsing garden catalogues in the winter. What do you
linger over? What do you order?

◈ Where do you garden? If you have experience with both
backyard and urban gardening, what do you like about each?
Which do you prefer?

◈ What fruits and vegetables do you grow? How do they compare
with store-bought?

◈ What's the most challenging thing you've ever tried to grow? Did you get it right?

◈ Tell me about the most fantastic crop you grew, or the most beautiful garden you ever planted and tended.

◈ Who, if anyone, gardens with you? Do you prefer to garden alone or with others? Why?

◈ When and how do you entertain in your garden?

◈ Describe a garden you'd consider enchanted. What are some of the loveliest gardens you've ever seen?

◈ If you've ever moved from a house where you'd tended a garden, how hard was it to leave behind the fruits of your labors? What cuttings or seeds did you take along with you?

◈ What is your favorite gardening book or author? What gardening philosophy have you picked up from your readings, and what philosophy do you pass along to others?

Collectors and Their Collections

◈ What kinds of things did you collect as a child, and how did you start? Where did you keep your collection?

◈ If someone started you on a collection when you were young, who was it and what did they give you? What do you remember about the first item you acquired?

◈ Are you still a collector? What are you looking for now?

◈ What led you to collecting? When did you begin?

◈ How do you decide what to collect? What draws you to a particular item?

◈ When and why did you get serious about your collection?

◈ How do you find things? Do you enjoy the hunt?

◈ Have you ever collected an item whose value greatly increased over time? Decreased? What have you bought or found that you thought was common but turned out to be really valuable? Do you shop with value in mind, or do you just buy what you like?

◈ What is your ultimate goal for your collection?

◈ What's your favorite kind of find—a complete set of related items, an item in perfect condition, or an item that's especially unique in some way?

◈ Have you ever felt that your collecting "bug" has gotten out of control? Have you ever run out of space? If so, what did you do?

◈ Have you ever tried to calculate how much money you've spent on your collection over your lifetime? What would you estimate that number to be? Do you consider it money well spent?

◈ What's your best find ever? What made it special? Where is it now?

◈ Have you ever broken or lost a favorite piece? What was it?

◈ What collections have you inherited?

◈ If you had to choose just one item to keep, what would it be?

◈ What constitutes a "collection"? How many pieces of a certain type of object make a collection—three or more? Or would you define a collection by some other criteria?

◈ What do you collect in a serious way? What do you collect in a casual way? What's the difference?

◈ What are the parameters you use for choosing the items you collect? For example, antique items at least one hundred years old?

◈ How do you feel about online auctions?

◈ How did the availability of the item you collect change as time went by?

◈ What kinds of collectors' organizations have you joined?

◈ In what ways did people who shared your collecting interest seem kindred spirits?

◈ How often do you "trade up" when you find a better version of something you already have? Why do you do this? What do you do with the item you're replacing?

◈ What causes you to lose interest in a collection or an item within a collection, and what do you do with items you no longer want?

◈ What discussions have you had with others about bequeathing your collections to a person or institution?

◈ If you have ever given a favorite piece away, to whom did you give it and why?

Artists and Artisans

◈ When and how did you first realize that you had a special talent for your art or a special interest in your craft?

◈ What materials, instruments, or other tools were available to you as a child? What materials do you most enjoy working with now?

◈ What inspires you? Nature? Your imagination?

◈ What sort of formal training did you receive early on?

◈ What teacher had the most influence on you? What artists have influenced you? What has been your greatest inspiration?

◈ What do you consider your first success as an artist, and in what ways did it change your life?

◈ When did you realize that your artistic endeavors would be your life's work? How did your family respond to your choice?

◈ What dramatic changes have you made in your work?

◈ What medium or performance style do you prefer?

◈ How do you feel about the body of work you've created so far in your life? What are the creative goals you have for your art?

◈ How would you describe your work to someone who had never seen it?

◈ With what arts communities have you been involved? How important have they been to you? What did you give to them, and what did they give to you?

◈ How does the public perception of your work affect you? How big a motivating factor are the opinions of others?

◈ What is the first music you remember hearing, the first song you remember singing, the first painting you remember loving?

◈ What were some of your first performances or exhibitions like?

◈ If you had your own band in high school, what did you play? Who were your bandmates? What kinds of gigs did you get and how much money did you make?

◈ What were some of the first concerts or exhibits you attended? Who was with you?

◈ Tell me about the instruments you've played in your life. How did you come to play them? What instruments would you like to learn to play?

◈ How does playing or dancing or painting or sculpting make you feel? How do you feel about performing for an audience?

◈ If you've been on the road, where have you gone and for how long? What is life like on the road?

◈ What dream have you yet to fulfill—composing an opera, dancing in a certain troupe, receiving recognition from a particular organization? What projects have you been dreaming of creating?

◈ What is your favorite time and place to write, paint, or practice? What's the strangest location in which you've worked?

◈ What do you see, hear, taste, smell, or feel as you create and work on your art or craft? Which of these senses is most important in your work?

◈ Whom do you most trust to provide early criticism of your work?

◈ What are some of the tools you use to overcome writer's block, performance anxiety, or stuck periods?

◈ What are your favorite venues in which to perform? Where have you performed most? Where would you like to perform in the future?

◈ In what ways do you belong to a community of artists?

◈ What's your favorite creation? Why? Who has it now?

◈ What was your most difficult or ambitious project?

Activists and Their Causes

◈ What enabled you to believe that you could or should make a difference?

◈ If your parents were activists, what were their causes, and how did they involve you?

◈ How has your personal experience motivated your activism? What have you seen in the world that impelled you to act? Can you identify a specific, perhaps spiritual, belief at the core of your desire to help?

◈ Through what channels do you find ways to take action?

◈ When did you begin to participate in your chosen cause?

◈ What issues draw you in the most—those you see, close to home, or those you hear about, far away?

◈ What was your first experience of volunteerism?

◈ What kind of role do you generally assume? Do you tend to work the "front lines" or stay behind the scenes?

◈ If you have ever participated in a demonstration, what was it like?

◈ How have you used civil disobedience as a tool of protest? Have you ever been arrested as a result? How do you feel about that experience now? Under what circumstances would you use civil disobedience again?

◈ What have you learned through your activism?

◈ What do you think you and the organizations you've been involved with have achieved for your cause? What was your greatest victory? Your most disappointing defeat?

◈ What are the rewards of your work?

◈ How have your interests changed over the years?

◈ In what ways has your involvement in this cause engaged your children in this or other causes?

◈ How worthwhile do you think your efforts have been?

◈ Do you feel you've helped change the world? How so?

"*Memory . . . is the diary that we all carry about with us.*"

—Oscar Wilde

Molding Your Material

Preparing & Preserving the Interview

YOU'VE PRESSED THE off button and packed up your things. You've gone home and had a listen—and it's real . . . you did it! You've captured the stories you wanted—and maybe you've gotten much, much more. Now what?

Don't just file away the treasure you worked so hard to unearth; find a way to keep your interview safe, and go one step further by turning it into a keepsake.

By definition, a "keepsake" is an object held onto for sentimental reasons. It's the kind of thing a cranky curmudgeon might call useless—but its purpose, its usefulness, is to serve as a physical reminder of a person, a time, or an experience.

Why not stop at the interview? Because now that you've saved your interviewee's stories in physical form, they depend on you for survival. Your role has evolved: You've graduated from cocreator to caretaker.

Whether you plan to deposit the recording in an archives or use it for a self-published family history, a video presentation, an online scrapbook, or any other creative project, you'll need to take care of a few things just after the interview. First, you'll jot down field notes in order to fill in important bits of interview context; then, you'll make copies of all materials so you'll have backup in case the originals are lost or damaged; finally, you'll begin to shape the content via indexing, transcribing, or editing. Oh, and don't forget to say thanks!

Show Your Appreciation

It may strike you as an old-fashioned gesture, but you really should thank your interviewee with a handwritten note. If you've planned multiple sessions, it doesn't hurt to send a note after each one (you can include a reminder of the date and time of your next get-together). You might acknowledge the loan of any documents and reassure the interviewee about when you intend to return them. The thank-you note is also a good place to confirm how the materials will be used and when the interviewee might expect to get copies of the recordings, transcripts, or projects (such as scrapbooks or scrapbook pages) you'll create.

> ### BORROWED DOCUMENTS
>
> If you've borrowed photographs, documents, or artifacts from your narrator or others, create a log and use it to keep track of what you have, to whom it belongs, when you received it, and when you'll return it.

Create Field Notes

Shortly after you have conducted an interview, you should make what professional oral historians call field notes: a written description of your surroundings and a summary of your interaction with the interviewee. (See page 172 for a Field Notes form.) If your interviewee gazed out the window at his rose garden while he spoke, jotting that down in your field notes will add context to his extended discussion of gardening. Even if no one but you and the interviewee ever listen to the recordings, these notes will help remind you of important details. Your field notes might include the following information:

❖ When the recording was made (date and time of day) and where. Who chose this time and place, and why?

❖ The environment in which the interview was conducted. How does it reflect your interviewee's background, tastes, living situation, or activities?

❖ What the two of you chatted about prior to or after the interview.

❖ If a third party was in the room, record his name and relationship to you or your interviewee and anything you feel his presence contributed to (or detracted from) the interview.

❖ Any interruptions that occurred—who interrupted, why, whether you stopped recording, and how long it took to get back to the interview.

How old were you when you got your first pet? Were you the one who took care of it?

❖ Any "off-the-record" exchanges—moments when the interviewee insisted that the recording device be turned off. While you shouldn't write down what was actually said, you can describe the topics that triggered the exchange.

❖ The interviewee's state of mind and physical condition—was he in top form, recovering from jet lag or an illness, anxiously awaiting a visit from an old friend, distraught about an upcoming move?

❖ If and when you are scheduled to meet with your interviewee again, and why.

Your interviewee may appreciate a copy of your field notes, but it's up to you to decide if you want to offer them to him. If he wants to add his own observations, have him add them on a separate sheet and attach it to your notes. Keep your field notes in a safe place with the original recordings and other documents.

Step One: Safeguard the Interview

Think about the recordings you have around your home—on LPs, audiotapes, CDs, DVDs, videotapes. First off, do you even know exactly where they are? Could they have been lost or misplaced during your last spring-cleaning or organizing binge, lent to that friend who moved to Montana? Even if you do know their whereabouts, do you know for sure that they're still in good condition? Maybe over the years your vinyl records have gotten scratched, or warped from heat or careless storage. Think of the cassette tapes left on the dashboard and stretched into unplayable lengths of audio spaghetti, the CDs sticky from soft drink spills or striated with invisible nicks.

You get the point: Most recording media is relatively fragile, and it doesn't help that we tend to treat it somewhat carelessly. Commercial recordings are pretty easy to replace, but an original interview recording is one of a kind. No story is told exactly the same way twice—in other words, were something to happen to your recording, it would be impossible to replicate the interview.

The simple act of duplication will greatly increase the chances that your interview will survive. How you go about it depends on your recording medium and on what kinds of future projects you intend to create.

Duplicating Tapes

The simplest way to have tapes copied is to send them to a duplication lab. (See "Resources" for some suggestions.) It's an expense, but it's worthwhile.

To do the duping yourself, you'll need two pieces of equipment: one to play the original recording and one to record onto. Recording technologies are in a constant state of evolution, so for copying instructions refer to your device's instruction manual or go online. Remember: You can transcribe text from tape copies, but you can't manipulate the recording itself; so if you want to create audio or video projects, you'll need to have your tapes transferred into digital form.

Going Digital

If you're starting digital (i.e., you used a digital camera or recorder), duplication is easy—given access to a computer, digital recorders are made to facilitate the downloading and reproduction of information. You may need a cable to connect the recorder to the computer or some additional equipment. Check your recorder's user manual for instructions.

If you're starting with tape or some other nondigital medium, you'll need to transfer the interview into digital form, aka "digitize" it. (This will enable you to create audio or video projects.) The transfer will require a special software program and various cables that may or may not have come with the recorder. Again, outsourcing may be the easiest way to go.

Whether you're making tape copies or digitized backups, the transfer process does take some time. (And if you plan on doing the duplication yourself, you should try it out on some test audio or video before breaking out the real thing—you wouldn't want to accidentally damage the recording or delete the files.)

Copy Your Digital Files

Though digital recorders often double as information storage units, you should download interviews as soon as possible after the interview. Take special precautions when saving files to your computer. You should be aware that internal hard drives can and do konk out. ("But I saved it to my hard drive!" is a forlorn plea computer technicians hear every day.) Invest in an external hard drive, or look into storing in a virtual hard drive. (Some people back up important files on more than one external hard drive.) Another good reason to do this is that video files in particular tend to take up a lot of memory and can slow down your computer.

How would you describe a perfect day? Who would be with you? What makes you happiest in life in general?

Once you're downloaded, make at least three sets of CDs or DVDs. Archival-quality CDs or DVDs are ideal, though more expensive. Often called "Archival Gold," they are designed to last much longer than regular CDs and DVDs; they're generally available from archival supply companies. (See page 177 for information on where to buy.). Designate each disc for one of the following uses:

❖ One is the "preservation" copy. If you can stand the expense, make this copy on archival-quality discs. Though this set won't technically be the original, you should treat it as such. Do not use it unless the files on your computer are no longer accessible or the other backup copies you made are damaged.

❖ One is the "access" copy. Use it for listening or viewing and for any projects you are planning to create based on your interview. For this copy you can use ordinary blank CDs and DVDs.

❖ One copy is for your interviewee. You may want to spring for archival-quality discs for this copy as well. Make additional copies to go wherever the two of you have agreed. (This has the added advantage of keeping one or more copies "off-site" for extra safety.)

Depending on your recorder's capacity, at some point you'll need to delete the original files in order to free up memory. Before you do, spot-check the file you have copied onto your hard drive or the

---

KEEPING UP WITH THE TIMES

From cave walls to pen and paper to laptop and beyond, technology is constantly evolving. But that doesn't mean we need to sacrifice our meaningful keepsakes to "progress" and relinquish them to obsolescence.

No matter how current a technology you use to record your interviews today, odds are pretty good that eventually it too will be obsolete. To keep the recordings of your interviews playable, you'll need to take note of new recording technologies and update your formats when necessary. (See page 178 for suggestions on where you can have materials transferred.) This may sound difficult, but ask anyone who has had their wonderful old home movies transferred to playable media—it can be done, and it's well worth the effort.

ALWAYS KEEP YOUR ORIGINALS— AND ALWAYS KEEP THEM SAFE

The whole world's gone digital and you carved your interview notes on a rock. Save the rock.

Or the mini-disc, the Super Eight reels, the audiocassettes. Never throw the original medium away. It has historical value, for one thing (if only as an artifact of the technology at the time of its creation). Maybe that rock will end up in a museum someday!

But perhaps more importantly for your purposes, it has integrity. It's the real thing—complete and authentic. You never know what can happen during duplication. Quality can suffer, sections can be jumbled or missed. The original is the "master recording," no matter how obsolete its technology may

become. For recordings "born digital," decide what you consider the original—a copy on an external hard drive, or a preservation CD or DVD (or perhaps both).

Treat your master recording as the precious artifact it is. Once you've copied it, put it away in a very safe space. The less it's handled, the less the potential for damage.

The Lesson

Use your backup copies, not your originals, for all listening or viewing and in the creation of any projects you undertake.

Don't use your original recordings unless the backup copies are damaged or lost.

CD you've designated for "preservation" to make sure everything seems okay. (If you have any doubts, listen to the entire thing.)

Copy Your Documents and Photographs

Once you've taken the first steps in safeguarding your recording, print out or copy any documents you created or collected over the course of the interview process—your question list, the completed Life History Worksheet and other forms, your field notes, any photographs taken at the interview, and any photographs or documents lent to you by the interviewee. Consider using archival quality paper and ink, available at scrapbooking stores, stationery stores, and online from archival supply companies; archival paper lasts much longer than regular paper and is usually described as "acid and lignin free."

Handle borrowed photographs and documents with special care, especially if you're dealing with originals. Any duplication process briefly puts the items at risk for loss or damage (especially if you use an outside copying service), so be sure to tell everyone

LABEL A PHOTO, SAVE A STORY

If you have a photograph that could benefit from some context, add what you know to your labeling. Maybe it's a photo of your interviewee's grandmother receiving her medical school degree; if she was the first woman at that school to earn such a degree, the image wouldn't be complete without a caption. Maybe you have a scanned copy of the deed to the Alderson family farm—but your interviewee doesn't use her maiden name. In a few years, you may not remember what that piece of paper has to do with Antoinette Suchow's interview. Write "Deed to Antoinette Suchow's (née Alderson) family farm" on the back of the document and you've saved a vital connection.

who handles your materials that they are precious originals and should be treated with extreme care. Return all borrowed items promptly, either in person or via a reliable carrier that provides tracking and delivery confirmation.

If you took any photographs on good old-fashioned film, have prints and scans made; back up digital photos on your computer, copy them onto CDs or DVDs, and make prints of your favorites. (You might want to include a few with your thank-you note to your interviewee.) Scan any borrowed photographs at home or at a photo lab and print out copies.

Back up digital documents onto CDs or DVDs (just as you did with the interview audio files), then print out at least two paper copies.

Preservation Know-How

It bears repeating: Now that you've captured a slice of history, you've got to do your part in keeping it safe. If you want to make sure your interview materials survive over the long haul, use archival supplies as you create and store them. Here are some more ways to help ensure their safekeeping:

❖ Keep your work surfaces clean. Always steer clear of food or liquids while working with interview materials.

❖ Handle photographs and documents by the edges. Never touch the front of a photograph with your fingers—oils from your skin can cause damage over time. Archivists wear simple white cotton gloves (available from vendors of archival supplies) when they handle photographs.

Do you remember whether your mother wore a particular perfume? What did it smell like?

❖ Beware of heat, humidity, and direct sunlight. A good gauge is to store your materials in an area where *you* would be comfortable—neither too hot or cold nor too damp.

❖ Store documents and photos in archival paper folders or archival plastic sleeves. (Look for polyester, polypropylene, or polyethylene—all plastics are not alike.)

❖ Store all components of the interview together in a clearly labeled archival folder, box, or binder.

❖ Label tapes, CDs, DVDs, or any recording media with the interviewee's name, your name, and the date and location of the recording. Use a solvent-free marker, available from suppliers of archival materials.

❖ Place CDs and DVDs in "jewel cases" or envelope enclosures (also clearly labeled) and store them with your paperwork.

❖ Label *copies* of borrowed photographs or documents with the name of the owner; that way you'll know whom to contact for more information, or for permission to reprint the material. Using a soft lead pencil, with very little pressure, write on the backs of photos or documents or on labels affixed to their protective storage sleeves. (Press hard and your writing may show through, permanently damaging the photo or document.) *Never* write directly on originals that have been loaned to you.

❖ Label photographs and documents with as much information as you have: names and dates, relationships, context, location, photographer, and so on. Again, use a soft lead pencil and write gently on the outer edges of the backs of your copies; never write directly on originals.

Step 2: "Decode" the Interview

"Have a listen!" You may be tempted to simply burn the interview onto some CDs and hand them out to close members of your family. That would certainly be the easiest way to share—but it's also the least enticing and effective. The recording includes all those stops and starts, pauses, off-topic asides, and throat clearings. Raw, unedited interviews can have their charms, but they're often maddeningly uneven—they may seem like treasures to you, but that's because you know what's in them. At the very least, you might just edit out the "dead air time"; but to really make the most of the interview, you should begin by indexing or transcribing the material into written form.

An index is a chronological synopsis of the interview, enabling you to quickly locate specific parts of the conversation on the recording. A transcript is a written copy of the interview; it can be read independent of the recording. Depending on what you'd like to do with your interview, you may need one or both.

Index the Interview . . .

Indexing is (by far) the less labor-intensive route, providing a map to your recordings rather than a detailed replica. It's a basic written outline of the interview, highlighting the major subjects discussed and indicating where in the recording they occur. An index can be as simple as a handwritten list of major topics, but typing it up will make it much more useful.

Don't strive to capture the exact words: Simply get the gist. Listen to the interview, breaking it down into relatively short chunks—of, say, five minutes—and briefly describing what was said during each of those periods. Small segments make for easier transcription and, ultimately, for more convenient reference.

If you're a very fast typist, you may not have a problem pounding out your notes as you listen; for the rest of us, it makes more sense to listen for a few minutes, pause the recording, take some notes, then start up again. (Some recording machines allow you to play back at slower speeds, a great boon during indexing.)

. . . Or Transcribe It

Transcribing is the translation of your recording into written form—the "transcript." You'll sit and listen to the interview and type out or handwrite what you hear. Do you need a transcript? If you are writing a family history, book, or article based on the interview, the answer is yes; if you are planning to edit your recording into an audio or video project, a transcript will help you locate the sections you want to include, but an index may work just as well.

Again, you'll probably need to work in small increments, pausing and playing back sections as many times as needed. Even if it's easier for you to handwrite the first version of your transcript, it will be worth your while to type it up; you'll be able to edit and format it, search through it by keyword, and share it via e-mail.

There are a variety of on-going debates concerning what constitutes "best practices" for transcriptions. Should you correct an interviewee's obvious "bad" grammar? How should you describe nonverbal audio, such as laughter or hesitation? When a person repeats phrases or entire thoughts, should the transcription include these repetitions? If the narrator has worded an answer in a confusing way, should it be corrected or clarified in the transcript?

Especially if you plan to participate in an oral history project with special guidelines, you may need to wrestle with such considerations. But if your interview is of a personal or familial nature, your "best practices" will probably reflect your goals. If you plan to provide access through an audio or video project, your transcript isn't the endgame and needn't be perfect. If you plan to write something, your transcript will be critical; the more information it captures, the more you'll have to work with.

If it's completeness you're after, begin with a first pass that's as true as possible to the recording, "warts" and all: the repeats,

Have you heard stories about what kind of baby you were—easy, finicky, a screamer?

the "bad" grammar, the "ummms," the confusing answers. Keeping a copy of the first pass intact, create an edited version that's more easily readable. (Read on for more on the editing process.)

Know that, as valuable a tool as your index or transcription will be, there is a limit to what it can describe. Even the most precise transcripts can't fully convey nuance: facial expressions and hand gestures, the way a person makes or fails to make eye contact, the pitch of the voice, the tone of a laugh. Document such cues by inserting notes into your transcript. "Long pause." "Sighs." "Giggling fit."

It may be helpful (and perhaps required by prior agreement) for you to give your interviewee a copy of the transcript to review. If the transcript is to be shared with a wide audience, it will be crucial—it's considered the interviewee's prerogative to correct grammar, remove repetition, make corrections, and otherwise edit the transcript, and you want to make sure he's happy with the final product. If you prefer, you can refine the transcript first and then ask your interviewee for his revisions.

There is no getting around the fact that the transcription process is labor intensive. It can take between six and twelve hours to transcribe a one-hour interview—plus hours more to edit and proofread it. So weigh your time constraints in determining how much you want to take on; you may want to start with the sections you found most compelling.

If your interview was recorded on audiocassettes, you might look into renting a transcription machine: a tape deck with a foot pedal

What are the traditional names in your family, the names that pop up generation after generation?

that allows you to control playback so you can stop, start, and reverse the tape hands-free while you type. Transcription and voice recognition software programs are also available—but if you've ever noticed the bloopers that turn up in the closed captioning of television shows, you know that you'll need to proofread the transcript very carefully! If your interview ran very long, you may want to look into having it professionally transcribed.

Editing the Interview

Editing is the process of selecting the parts of your interview you feel are most important, interesting, or suitable for sharing, and then bringing those sections together to create a condensed version of the narrative.

Text, audio, and video can all be edited, depending upon your access to the necessary equipment.

For text editing, you can start from either a transcript or an index. A transcript can be condensed, and an index can be expanded—you'd go back and transcribe the sections you want to share. In either case, the goal is to fashion the parts into a cohesive document. If you want to incorporate

With what economic group did your family identify? Has your perception of that changed over time?

photographs and miscellaneous documents, you can scan them and place them in the appropriate points in the edited text. (More on that in chapter 5.)

To edit audio and video recordings in their original media, you'll need to invest in specialized editing software—and you'll need to learn how to use it. For audio recordings, you should be able to find free programs online; try Audacity. For video, you can explore evolving open source programs or look into purchasing a software program such as iMovie, Adobe Final Cut Express, Pinnacle Studio Ultimate, or Adobe Premiere Elements; the choice will depend on the type of computer you're working with and on what kinds of bells and whistles you're looking for. *A note:* If you have never done any audio or video editing before, you might ask a techie friend for help or pay a professional to walk you through the process.

Use your transcript or index as a guide while you edit: A printout will make it easy to locate the specific portions of the recording you're searching for.

A SAMPLE INTERVIEW INDEX AND TRANSCRIPT

◆

What follows are examples of how one portion of an interview has been indexed, transcribed, and edited. As regards the index in particular, you may already have your own note-taking style; but this sample will give you a sense of the level of detail for which you should be aiming. Likewise, in the edited transcript the interviewer's questions have been omitted, and the interviewee's answers woven into a narrative; that's one approach, but it's by no means the only way.

PARTIAL INDEX

◆

Time Stamp	Topics
1:32–4:45	Born into farming family in Norwich, CT. Father had the family dairy farm. When she was 10 moved to another farm—dad used horses for farm work, not machinery. It was fun to grow up on farm, helped father do his work. Chores? Lots of chores. When he cultivated corn she would drive horse to help him, she rode on horse—would daydream and steer horse onto corn. Worked hardest when they were haying. Would drive the team. Haying dependent on weather.

UNEDITED TRANSCRIPT

◆

INTERVIEWER: Tell us a little bit about the family into which you were born.

INTERVIEWEE: I was born into a farming family in Norwich, Connecticut. My father had a small dairy farm. Actually he had the family farm. And then when I was about ten we moved to a bigger farm where he had a few more cattle. And he was very old-fashioned in that he loved working with animals. And we always had horses, for years and years, and not any tractor. And that was one thing I grew up doing, I learned at an early age how to drive a team of horses. And it was a fun thing to grow up on a farm because you were outside a lot. And there were just my sister and I so that I helped my dad a lot.

INTERVIEWER: Did you have chores around the farm?

INTERVIEWEE: Oh, yes, lots of chores . . . I helped my father. He always cultivated his corn after it was planted and that was a big thing. And I would drive one horse to help him when he was holding the cultivator. I rode on the horse to drive it. I did that year after year—every once in a while I'd start to daydream and I would not steer it and I'd drive the horse on the row of corn. He would not be too happy with me. (Laughs.) I just did a lot of things. Some gardening. I guess when I worked the most and the hardest was in the summertime when we were haying. I usually drove the horses in the team wagon while the hay loader was loading hay and my father stood on the load of hay and evened things out. It was a fun job but we were always . . . because haying depends on the weather you were always hoping that you were going to have lots of sunny days to get the hay dry and in.

EDITED TRANSCRIPT

◆

I was born into a farming family in Norwich, Connecticut. My father had the family farm. When I was about ten we moved to a bigger farm where he had a few more cattle. He was very old-fashioned in that he loved working with animals and we always had horses and didn't have a tractor. It was a fun thing to grow up on a farm because you were outside a lot. There were just my sister and I so I helped my dad a lot.

I learned at an early age how to drive a team of horses. My father always cultivated his corn after it was planted and I would drive one horse to help him when he was holding the cultivator. I rode on the horse to drive it and every once in a while I'd start to daydream and wouldn't steer it. I'd drive the horse onto the row of corn!

I guess when I worked the most and the hardest was in the summertime when we were haying. I usually drove the horses in the team wagon while the hay loader was loading hay and my father stood on the load of hay and evened things out. It was a fun job but you were always hoping that you were going to have lots of sunny days to get the hay dry and in.

—from Lisa Samson's interview with Jeanne R. Jatkowski, October 2005

"*Right now a moment is fleeting by! Capture its reality in paint!*"

—Paul Cezanne

Turning It Into Something More

Writing, Scrapbooking & Archiving Your Interview

O NCE YOU'VE GOTTEN the story down, the creative possibilities are endless. Your interview can be preserved as a historical document in a family archives, local history association, library, or oral history project; it can also be given as a timeless gift to family and friends. Here are a few projects and approaches to consider.

❖ Print out copies of interview transcripts on acid-free paper and present them in custom-decorated archival-quality envelopes or boxes.

❖ Burn (that is, copy) edited versions of the original recording on archival-quality "gold" CDs or DVDs and enclose them in decorative sleeves.

❖ Make scrapbooks (or a scrapbook page), combining excerpts from the interview transcript with photographs, journal entries, and decorative embellishments. (See pages 146 to 154.)

❖ Use calligraphy (or hire a calligrapher) to hand letter a favorite interview passage or quotation on archival paper; or needlepoint, cross-stitch, or embroider a brief passage into a pillow or other decorative keepsake.

❖ Use interview content as a resource for all sorts of writing projects.

Using Your Interview as Writing Material

Many people embark on personal interviews with the express goal of creating a written work—whether what they have in mind is an article or report, a novel, a memoir, or a biography. If you've toyed with the notion but are intimidated, read on—you may think that a short story or a novel is far beyond your abilities, but if you're prepared to devote the time and energy, it's worth a try.

Everyone has the right to write. Why we don't *all* write more often about our lives and thoughts is something of a mystery. Even people with no special training can write an interesting and informative piece, as long as they're willing to bone up on the basics of good form and style. You may need a bit of a refresher course in grammar and punctuation. Consider taking a writing class, joining a writers' group, or picking up a reference book to improve your skills and bolster your confidence.

If you'd like to try writing something but are stuck on what exactly it should be, here are some projects to consider.

❖ A retelling of one of your interviewee's stories. Don't feel as though you have to write up your interviewee's entire life path. Why not choose one special anecdote, adding background and details to round it out?

❖ An introduction to the interview. Explain why and how you created it, and append the document to the transcript or add it to the edited recording.

❖ A complete biography of your interviewee. A challenging endeavor that can stretch out for years, the task of writing a biography is not to be taken lightly.

❖ The story of the planning and recording of the interview. In some cases, this may be a key piece of the puzzle. How did you feel about the interview, and what did you learn from it? What surprised or inspired you?

❖ A cookbook. Did your interview yield recipes? Consider adding an introduction describing how you got the recipes (maybe you prepared the dish alongside the contributor) and why and how you conducted the interviews. Write an introductory paragraph for each recipe (perhaps in collaboration with the interviewee) detailing its history or offering helpful preparation tips.

❖ A work of fiction. From poems to short stories, novellas, and novels, creative possibilities abound.

❖ An overview of a group of interviews. If you've interviewed several members of the same family or of some other type of group, combine and compare their voices. Put like questions together in chronological order, and you'll end up with a document that reveals the evolution of a group's traditions or a family's values.

❖ Supplementary material contextualizing the interview. You can incorporate such material into your transcript, making sure it's clearly differentiated from the text of the interview. Or you can treat it as a "script": Record yourself reading it aloud, and then use an audio editing program to add it to the edited recording.

❖ Individual letters to accompany the recording. If you're giving a version of the recording to your children, siblings, or other family members, write and attach personal letters.

Writing Tips

Thinking that you can't write *well* can stop you from trying to write *at all.* The idea that your story or poem or essay must be perfect may be enough to deter you from putting your thoughts on paper. The fact is, though, that if you can think it or say it, you can write it. If you want to write but are tangled up in reasons not to, the following techniques can help you sidestep your fears and get started.

Use Flow Writing to Practice

"Flow writing" is the process of uninterrupted, uncensored writing. The approach is meant to put you in touch with your thoughts and get you comfortable with the physical act of writing; it's not about the quality of the results.

Start with a blank notebook or pad of paper if you prefer to write by hand, or open a new computer document if you're more accustomed to typing. Set a timer for thirty minutes. For the practice run, you needn't limit yourself to subjects related to the interview; focus on any person, thing, event, or experience you feel like writing about—and just start. Put down anything that comes to mind: factual information, random associations, emotions, and memories. Again, don't censor yourself; the point of the exercise is to write without interruption.

For now, don't worry about punctuation, spelling, grammar, or structure: Corrections, additions, and revisions can all come later. Now is the time to let your mind take you where it will. Follow your thoughts wherever they go, and try to stay out of the way. Work as fast as you can, and don't stop until the time is up.

When did you really know that you wanted to spend the rest of your life with this person?

If you feel ready to work on shaping your interview material, focus on a specific situation—say, your mother's experience at her senior prom. Use your mother as the subject of a round of flow writing; then set the timer again and use a different perspective, this time writing about the room, the decorations, the music, and so on. Let the material sit for a bit, then come back to it. Start editing and rewriting, and odds are you'll be surprised by the amount of valuable stuff you find there.

Focus In

No matter how grand your ambitions for your project, don't let the big picture overtake you. The greatest achievements are built on a series of small steps. Start by focusing in on some of the smaller details—a man's description of his first suit, a childhood game.

Especially if you're writing fiction, those details may come at unexpected times. They may arise from your flow writing or while you're listening to a recording or reading a transcript; or an

CLARIFY YOUR INTENTIONS

There are many ways to use interview materials as a springboard to writing—but before you go down a particular road, consider some questions:

❖ If you're writing fiction, will you hew fairly closely to the life of your interviewee, or will you spin a fantasy based on some of his stories? If the former, will you take care to disguise identities and places?

❖ If it's nonfiction, will it use the transcript as the primary source, with certain facts or background material added for context? Or will it contain statements from others about the interviewee, including their recollections as well?

❖ How extensive is the project? Are you focusing on one story or one person's life, or will you attempt to trace a group history?

❖ Who is your audience? Do you intend to print out your piece for family members only, as a gift for a family reunion or special celebration, for instance? A wider audience? If so, who?

❖ How much time are you willing to devote to the project? When must it be (or would you like it to be) finished? Could it take months or years to complete? Are you comfortable with this time frame?

❖ Do you have your interviewee's written approval to use his life stories or other interview materials in this manner? If you already have permission, go ahead, but if you're not sure, discuss the planned project with your interviewee before you start writing, or get an opinion about your rights (per your written usage agreement) from a qualified attorney.

PUBLISHING ON THE WEB: A RISKY PROPOSITION

One seemingly straightforward (and temptingly easy) way to provide access to an interview is to post all or part of your digitized recordings on a secure, private website. But there's no guarantee that the materials you post will remain "secure and private" for long (perhaps not more than a few seconds!).

In our digital world, it's so easy to distribute audio and video files instantly, around the planet. Websites like Facebook and YouTube encourage us to post personal information about ourselves, and you may feel tempted to share your interviewee's recorded personal history in this way. But unless you have a written agreement that allows you to use all or part of the interview in this fashion, *it's not right to do so*—for both ethical and legal reasons. Be wary of posting interview content on public websites in general, especially considering the concerns people have these days about identity theft.

It's best to consider all interviews confidential conversations, not something that either participant would necessarily expect or wish to share publicly on the Web. A much safer way to distribute the materials electronically is to e-mail them as attachments to specific individuals, with instructions about how the material can and should be used.

association might be jogged by an unrelated image or object. Facts, ideas, and phrases may pop into your head at any time—when you're listening to music, cooking, walking. So keep pen and paper handy at all times, and write down those fleeting thoughts; later, organize your notes and add information as it comes to mind (or as you discover it through research). Eventually, you'll create larger pieces by combining these small, focused units.

You can also work to gather these details. Say you want to write about the life of a gardener you know. You could approach your research in a variety of ways. You might sit in a garden (any garden, but hers if possible) for an hour or two to get a sense of what her experience was like; if there are gardeners working there, all the better—watch them. You might do some searching in a library or online, whether you're after a larger context or an accurate illustration of a beloved rose. All these bits and pieces could come together in an essay called "A Life in the Garden."

This tight-angle view is not the only way to work, but for many writers it's the most approachable.

Rewrite, Sleep on It, and Rewrite Again

A great deal of amateur writing is unclear, awkward, or boring simply because the writer hasn't worked on it long enough. It's hard to imagine any writer getting everything down perfectly in a first draft. Professional writers rewrite and revise repeatedly, working like sculptors to cut away everything that isn't part of the final form they want to reveal.

It's very easy to edit your work on a computer, but you may want to keep each draft as a separate document in case you later want to reinstate something you've edited out. Or start a

What are the memorable stories in your family, those that are passed on and told again and again? Who told them to you, and who tells them best?

"spare parts" document or folder where you can tuck away the portions of text you delete. During the rewriting process, you're sure to find a word, sentence, paragraph, or even an entire chapter that isn't quite right, doesn't make sense anymore, doesn't ring true, or doesn't contribute to the flow of your piece (even if it seemed brilliant when you first wrote it). Don't hesitate to delete it—just do it and move on. Print out each draft as you complete it and leave it for a day or two. When you review the piece, you'll be amazed at how different it can seem with a fresh perspective. Rewrite as many times as you need to—a dozen times is not too many—refining and clarifying with each revision. When you think the piece is finished, read it aloud to yourself and others to be sure that you've been totally clear, included all the important details, and created something you can be proud of.

Printing and Distributing Your Writing

If you're looking to bind your writing into book form or to distribute more copies than you care to make at home, get thee to a printer—there are good ones in most towns and cities nationwide. Check with your friends or business associates for their recommendations, and do some comparison shopping. Look at

Who in your family do you most resemble? Do you recognize your parents in some of your mannerisms or expressions?

samples and get price quotes for your specific printing project. Go online to compare the features and prices offered by national companies that specialize in photo-book publishing; some of these companies actually provide downloadable software programs to help you create your finished books.

A note on reducing costs: If the estimates you receive seem high across the board, you may need to alter your project to fit your budget. The size of a printer's press often dictates the number of pages that can be printed in one "print run" or batch. He may have to charge you substantially more for printing just a few extra pages if your job doesn't fit his standard forms. You may be able to avoid these extra charges just by talking to your printer and editing your manuscript to a more cost-effective page count. On the flip side, color printing varies in price; you might be able to get two ink colors rather than one at little additional cost if you query your printer and find that his press can handle both colors in one pass. Submitting your manuscript and artwork digitally rather than on paper may save you a considerable amount of money, too.

Before you give any printing project to a printer, designer, bookbinder, or paper supplier, make sure you discuss and understand all your options and the total costs for your project.

Scrapbooking Your Interview

Whether you're new to scrapbooking or an avid practitioner, the relatively accessible craft may be the perfect way to get creative with your interview. The interplay of words and images can give a story unparalleled immediacy—and that immediacy will be especially appealing if you're looking to transform the interview into a gift or keepsake.

If you have access to a trove of photographs, use them! Alongside excerpts that give voice to their stories, the subjects in those photographs will come to life. Behind-the-scenes tales, little-known facts, and even the most ordinary captions ("Sharyn P., Los Angeles, 1973") will contextualize photos. And it works the other way around, too: The photos enhance the transcript. It's the same

WHAT IS SCRAPBOOKING?

The word *scrapbooking* crept into common American usage during the early 1990s, when the centuries-old pastime mushroomed into a national craze.

Just as with handmade quilts, the imaginative use of decorative techniques, patterns, and color combinations can elevate a scrapbook from humble to museum-worthy. And just like quilts, scrapbooks have a long and storied history: Many Victorian-era scrapbooks (circa 1860–1900) still survive in museum and library collections, a poignant reminder of the form's multifaceted past.

Unlike today's iterations, though, the scrapbooks of this period did not typically house photographs; family photos were stored in separate albums. The books tended to be decorated with eclectic combinations of colorful images.

In a way, scrapbooks were a sign of the times. In the late 1860s, technological advances had made commercial color printing much more affordable, which allowed scrapbook-making to take off. Elegant gold-stamped fabric- and leather-bound albums with rag-paper pages were lovingly filled with brightly colored, intricately die-cut embossed paper "scraps" and other printed ephemera. The manufactured scraps came in a wide range of sizes and featured images of flowers, animals, people in costume, and a myriad of other subjects.

By the 1880s, small, colorful "trade cards" were readily given away by manufacturers seeking to promote their wares (one of the first advertising gimmicks ever). Their sentimental or comical designs were avidly collected by both rich and poor. Chromolithographed album cards and plates from seed catalogues, color inserts from magazines and newspapers, and sundry other paper goods were coveted as well; images of fruits and flowers and fashionable ladies were carefully cut out and glued in artful arrangements in many period scrapbooks.

Though scrapbook-making is now more popular than ever before, in truth, the current scrapbooking "movement" has no real historical precedent—for scrapbooks have never been quite so public as they are now. Today's scrapbook as family documentary is a modern medium of expression—essentially a new way of documenting history and sharing life stories, one pretty page at a time.

principle you followed in labeling your photographs (see page 130), but when you're scrapbooking, you make those connections plain for all to see.

The process can be as straightforward or involved as you like. For a relatively simple take, you can slip a copy of the interview recording or transcript into a decorative envelope and attach it to the inside cover of a scrapbook pasted full of photos with brief captions. If you want to illustrate an entire transcript, that's going to take a bit more doing—but the odds are pretty good that you'll end up with something really special.

The possibilities are endless. You can use a portion of your transcribed interview as a banner headline or title. You can match single interview questions and answers with particular photographs. You can select one or more evocative phrases or passages and repeat them continuously, creating a patterned background for your photographs. In fact, given a simple word-processing application of the type found on virtually every computer, you can use size, color, and font to transform the text of your interview into endless decorative variations. (And if you're familiar with more complex computer design and layout programs such as Adobe InDesign or Photoshop or have access to scrapbooking software, you'll be able to create elaborate, multilayered compositions.)

Some people love poring over pictures and working on layouts and others can't find the time. There are plenty of options here for every level of involvement—and before you bite off more than you can chew, keep in mind that a single beautiful page can be just as meaningful a gift as an album filled with many complicated pages.

Your Scrapbooking Goal

The best way to begin a scrapbook is to figure out why you want to make it. Think through your motivations: how you envision using the scrapbook, where you imagine it might take up permanent residence, and with whom you'd like to share it. If you plan to offer a digitally reproduced keepsake to everyone at your grandfather's eightieth birthday bash, maybe you'd make it short and sweet; not all fifty guests will be interested in a detailed time line of your grandfather's life, and you have to think about the expense of reproducing a hefty book. Maybe you'd want to focus the subject, choosing a topic you think most everyone might be able to relate to (your grandfather's cooking stories and recipes, for instance).

What talents or interests did your parents bring into the life of the family?

Once you've clarified your intentions, figure out what type of album and page size you think will best suit the photographs, text, and any other materials you'd like to use. To ensure that your creations survive the test of time, always use archival materials.

Organize Your Photos

Before you start making page layouts, gather and organize your photographs. You can arrange them by theme, year, or person or according to the projects you have in mind. Keep smaller photos in acid-free sleeves (Mylar is worth looking for) in photo storage boxes with tab dividers; larger ones (in protective sleeves) will fit in an archival storage box.

While you're going through photographs, be attuned not only to your sorting, but also to design inspiration. Any number of things can spark page treatments—the color of a loved one's hair, a photograph of a favorite garden . . .

Scan the photographs you want to work with or have them scanned at a copy or photo shop; once they're on your computer, you'll easily be able to manipulate their size and crop them as desired (and if you're handy with photofinishing techniques, you'll be able to perform all kinds of decorative trickery). You can work with photocopies or prints, but you'll lose some degree of flexibility. Again: Don't use original photographs unless you intend to use your project as the long-term storage place.

Storybook or Picturebook? Choose Your Format

Will you make a "storybook" or a "picturebook"? A *storybook-style* scrapbook centers around text: Portions of the transcript fill most of each page and are accompanied by related pictures to illustrate

CHOOSE YOUR TOOLS AND MATERIALS

As you shop for albums, paper, inks, pens, and ornaments, choose materials to complement the colors, textures, and subjects of your photos and documents. Stay on track with your color scheme so your materials coordinate nicely when you start putting the book together. And try not to go overboard when purchasing three-dimensional embellishments; you can always get more later.

That's the fun stuff, but the right tools are what will give you the most polished results. Here's a basic inventory of scrapbooking items:

❖ A pair of small, sharp scissors

❖ Metal straight-edge

❖ Transparent plastic ruler

❖ X-acto blade holder, blades, and a cutting mat, or you can use a paper trimmer instead

❖ Soft lead pencil and large, soft eraser

❖ Journaling pens (acid-free, archival quality, lightfast, and nonbleeding)

❖ Photo mounting squares and/or adhesive-backed photo corners

❖ A roll of double-sided scrapbooking tape and a roll of removable tape

❖ Acid-free, photo-safe archival glue in both stick and liquid forms (look for a pointed applicator tip)

the interviewee's life stories. In a *picturebook-style* scrapbook, photographs and other visuals are used more prominently; relatively brief excerpts from the transcripts are featured as captions, copy blocks, and headlines to enhance or complete the visual narrative. If you only have access to a few photographs, storybook would be the way to go; if you or the interviewee wants to showcase a fascinating collection of images or only wants to share a small portion of the interview, a picturebook might facilitate these aims.

Choose Your Page Size

There are three standard page sizes made to fit most scrapbook albums: 8" × 8", 8½" × 11", and 12" × 12". (Both solid-colored and preprinted decorative papers come in all three sizes.) If you're not familiar with these standard page sizes or with scrapbooking supplies in general, make a preliminary visit to a craft or scrapbooking store before taking the plunge.

Lay two same-size sheets of paper side by side to see how they'll look as a spread (two facing pages). The 8" × 8" pages make 8" × 16" spreads; these are often used in gift books that focus on a single event or person, as the small size suggests intimacy. Two 12" × 12" pages make spacious 12" × 24" spreads roomy enough for large photos and lots of embellishments. The advantage of working with 11" × 17" spreads (two 8½" × 11" sheets) is that they are perfect for standard home office printers, but this size can be a little tight for layouts with lots of photos.

After you select your page size, lay in a sufficient supply of blank pages and buy (or make) an album. Choose a good quality album and paper—this is not a place to skimp. Looseleaf albums accommodate three-dimensional items well, are convenient if you want to move pages around, and lie flat when open (with a space between the facing pages). "Post-bound" albums give spreads a more seamless appearance, like the pages in a bound book.

A Storybook Scrapbook

Begin planning out your storybook page designs by experimenting with practice layouts. When you're trying things out on your computer, be sure to safeguard the integrity of your files by cutting and pasting material from the digital version of your transcript into a new, "working" document.

❖ Start with the format. Select page margins on all four sides, then copy and paste in a portion of your transcript to fiddle with. Select a few fonts you like and experiment with them on-screen in different sizes and styles (bold, italic, and so on). Play with your images, too, enlarging them, reducing them, or cropping away uninteresting or unwanted elements.

Reduced

Enlarged

Silhouetted

Cropped

There were two generations of cowboys in my family, grandfather Wyatt Garrison in the 1880s, and my brother Joe

Storybook scrapbooks offer opportunities to play with text via column width and length, font size and style, and various color combinations.

- ❖ When you've settled on some favorite fonts and image sizes, print out samples on letter-size copier paper. (If you have a color printer or access to one, you might play around with font color as well.) Make note of which fonts and styles you're working with so you don't forget!

- ❖ Neatly trim around your blocks of text.

- ❖ Lay out four or six scrapbook pages in two-page spreads, and place your text blocks on the spreads. In the empty spaces, try a few different image arrangements. Don't glue anything down yet—these are just experimental layouts; if you wish, you can hold things in place with small bits of Scotch removable transparent tape (it has a blue core).

❖ Experiment with other layout designs: type positions; columns of type 3 or 6 inches wide; phrases and quotes used as headlines; blocks of copy in various shapes and sizes; or text running only across the bottom halves of the pages, with pictures filling the top halves. In a word-processing document, you can achieve most of these type effects by arranging transcript portions in various shapes and sizes, printing them on paper, then cutting out the text as desired.

❖ Once you feel comfortable playing with text, begin work on your final layouts. Choose a single font—this strong design mechanism will help the story flow from page to page. (Multiple fonts can be distracting.) For variety, you'll still have the option of working with color, size, and spacing for creative effect. For instance, all questions could appear in green 10-point type, with answers in black 12-point type; certain important phrases and words could be highlighted in red or blue or set in a larger font size. You might spice things up a little with *one* additional font that's reserved for headlines and titles only.

❖ Print out parts of the transcript (on archival-quality paper in white or appropriate colors) to fit the first spread and for each sequential page or spread of your scrapbook; carefully trim

---

THREE SCRAPBOOKING COMMANDMENTS

1. Use archival-quality supplies.

2. Be as careful and neat as you possibly can (let inks dry thoroughly to control smudges, and avoid glue drips and overflow).

3. Use archival-quality copies rather than original vintage photos and documents on your pages—*unless* you intend the scrapbook to be the permanent home for your originals, in which case you should put them in transparent archival plastic or Mylar sleeves and attach these—not the photos themselves—to the pages.

PAPER, SCISSORS, GLUE

The use of various design software programs can eliminate much of the handwork entailed in scrapbooking. Such programs can be expensive and often involve a hefty learning curve; so if you're a novice, you may be better off sticking to (relatively) old-fashioned tools like word-processing programs and scissors and glue.

(leaving about ¼" of blank space on all sides) and position the text printouts in attractive arrangements with photographs, ephemera, documents, and decorative embellishments.

❖ Use archival photo-mounting squares to attach photographs, and double-faced scrapbooking tape or small amounts of archival-quality acid-free glue for printed text blocks and other items.

A Picturebook Scrapbook

Picturebook scrapbooks showcase photographs on every page, using text in more of a decorative role.

❖ To begin planning your picturebook spreads, assemble all available photos of the person you interviewed, as well as those relating to the content of the interview, and try to match them up with the text of your transcript.

❖ In this kind of scrapbook, photos will take up a much larger percentage of each page than text, so the snippets of text that explain the pictures should be either concisely informative or particularly meaningful. As you sort and match photos to stories, use a highlighting pen to mark interesting parts of the text on a working copy of the transcript.

❖ Work out a few trial arrangements on your page spreads. Try using transcript excerpts as headlines, and see how your copy blocks look in a variety of sizes, fonts, and colors. You may want to enlarge, crop, or reduce certain photos.

❖ Position photographs beside text printouts, ephemera, and decorative embellishments as desired for final layouts. As you work, consider how each two-page spread will flow with the rest of the book, and remember to be true to the original meaning of your interviewee's words as you edit and excerpt the transcript.

❖ Use archival photo-mounting squares to attach photographs, and double-faced scrapbooking tape or small amounts of archival-quality acid-free glue for printed text blocks and other items.

Picturebook scrapbooks invite thematic combinations of photographs and significant interview excerpts, which may be set in text blocks of various shapes and sizes.

The Album Cover

The old saying "Never judge a book by its cover" probably came about because people *do* judge books by their covers. Make yours compelling by customizing it with colorful and evocative details. A ribbon tie might be all that's needed to dress up a plain album, but you may want to go for an aesthetic overhaul. You might wrap the entire cover in bright fabric or even cover it with a portion of the transcript, printed on sturdy but flexible archival paper. A single photograph, framed on the front cover, might serve to introduce the subject of the book. The cover can hint at the style and look

The outside of a scrapbook can be personalized and embellished with ornamentation, text, and imagery. Go bold or keep it simple.

of the interior pages or reflect the unique personality of its subject. Add decorative endpapers to catch the eye as the book is opened.

Adding a Recording of the Interview

Want to include a copy of your interview recording with your scrapbook? Easy enough: Simply place the disc in a store-bought, archival CD/DVD envelope, and attach it to the scrapbook's inside front cover with double-sided scrapbooking tape or photo-mounting squares. If you prefer, you can also create a custom-made decorative folder to house it. You'll need:

- A sheet of solid-color or patterned archival-quality cardstock or other heavy paper at least 7" tall and 15" long
- Soft lead pencil
- Metal straight-edge
- X-acto knife
- Acid-free paper glue
- Double-sided archival tape
- Velcro "dot" closure (optional)

1. Draw a rectangle measuring 6½" × 14½" on the cardstock. Holding it horizontally, mark vertical fold lines 5½" from the left edge and 3½" from the right edge.

14½"

6½"

Step 1A

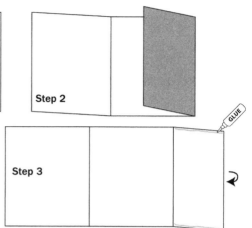

5½"   5½"   3½"

6½"

Step 1B

Step 2

Step 3

2. Cut out the rectangle. *Lightly* score the fold lines and fold the flaps inward; the narrower flap forms a pocket to hold the disc, and the wider one forms a cover flap.

3. Apply a thin bead or drop of glue along the top and bottom inside edge of the narrower flap and let the glue set momentarily before you glue down the flap (be sure to glue edges only, leaving enough room to insert a computer disc). Let the glue dry thoroughly.

4. Attach decorative embellishments, a photo, or a title treatment to the front panel.

Grandfather John Herd
INTERVIEW 2009

Step 4   Step 5

5. If desired, center a Velcro dot under the cover flap. Attach it with its own self-adhesive backing or with a few drops of glue.

Use double-sided tape to attach the folder to the inside front cover of your scrapbook. Insert disc.

Decorative Presentation Boxes

If you're planning on turning your interview into a gift, presentation counts. A special box will make your package feel like more of a treasure.

Make sure that it's a comfortable fit: You should be able to easily remove and replace your scrapbook, transcript, or disc (or any combination thereof) without damaging it. Measure the item(s), then shop for or make a box or other container with an interior dimension that will leave you with at least ¼" clearance on all sides. If you intend to use the presentation box as permanent storage, go archival. If you want to use a nonarchival container (a wooden crate, a cookie tin, or a cardboard box, for example), use archival glue to line it with archival paper (the paper will create a protective barrier) and/or insert the materials into protective Mylar sleeves or archival envelopes before you put them in the container.

Archiving Your Interview

While it may require a leap of faith to imagine that your interview will be of interest to listeners in 150 years, you never know. You've recorded a piece of oral history. Its broader relevance may escape you, but picture this: In March 2008, attendees at the annual meeting of the Association for Recorded Sound Collections were treated to the first public playback of an audio recording made in April of 1860—the year Abraham Lincoln was first elected president. The recently rediscovered recording, created on an invention called the phonautograph, featured the inventor singing a portion of the French song "Au Clair de la Lune."

Not a famous person's voice. Just that of someone singing a tiny snippet of song. But the ordinary becomes extraordinary in the wider context of history: *This* person is singing on what is thought to be the first documented recording of a recognizable human voice.

THINK AHEAD

If possible, contact active oral history projects before you start recording your interviews. Many projects that accept interviews created by the public at large will take materials only if they conform to specific technical guidelines; look into requirements and seek guidance if needed.

Timing may be a factor, too: Projects typically collect materials for a finite period, after which their holdings are archived. If you can't find an active oral history project that suits you, look into donating your materials to an archives instead. (See page 160 for more on how to choose one.)

More to the point: Preservation is what enabled the recording to survive. The phonautograph's inventor, Édouard-Léon Scott de Martinville, deposited his recording at the French Academy of Sciences as part of his patent application—and that institution maintained it and kept it safe.

As caretaker of your recording, you too must make decisions about its future: in what form you will preserve the recorded materials, where you will store them, how you will organize them, how you will share the information within them with others, and how you will plan for their future.

Where do you go when you want solitude? Have you ever traveled alone? What was that like for you?

The Wider Relevance of Your Interview

Although all interviews are precious in some way, not every recording will require an equal level of continuing care or access. It's up to you to weigh the value of the stories you have recorded—to yourself and your narrator, to your family and friends, and to the wider community. This assessment will determine the appropriate care and distribution of the recordings and documents.

Recordings of a personal and sentimental nature—your grandfather telling stories of teenage pranks, your young niece talking about her recent summer vacation—certainly deserve basic safekeeping and informal sharing. You'll fulfill your caretaker role by storing such recordings in your home and sharing them with family or friends—and eventually, by making a decision about passing them on.

Other recordings cry out for a larger audience. The stories of individuals who've lived through important historical periods or events or who are members of underdocumented groups may prove invaluable to researchers. A man who worked as a steelworker during the 1970s might provide a very personal glimpse into the

INTERVIEWING PROSPECTIVE "HOMES"

There are many pluses to donating to an archives or participating in an oral history project, but you'll want to be sure that you select an organization whose goals and values are in line with what you and your interviewee have in mind.

Before making a commitment, be sure to look into the following:

❖ What is the main purpose of the oral history project or the collecting policy of the archives?

❖ Who is the intended audience and who is allowed access to the materials?

❖ What restrictions are or can be placed on access and use of the content of interviews?

❖ What types of recordings are accepted—audio only, or video as well? Is one medium preferred?

❖ How are materials accessed?

❖ What are the guidelines for submission?

❖ Is an index or transcript required?

❖ What type of legal releases are required? Will the institution provide them?

❖ *For an oral history project:* Where will the original recordings and related interview materials be archived? Who is in charge of these archives?

❖ *For an oral history project:* Is any interview support provided? Is it possible to borrow equipment, for instance?

Note: *Retain a copy of any materials you place on deposit. You want to be sure you'll always have easy access.*

---

decline of American steel manufacturing. Your next-door neighbor, displaced as a result of the Vietnam War, may reveal a new facet in the ever-evolving story of the Vietnamese boat people.

If you believe that your interview recordings include this sort of significant material, consider participating in an oral history project or donating your completed interviews to an institutional archives. Your long-term caretaker responsibilities will be transferred to this project or institution, and the materials will be safely preserved and accessible to researchers well into the future.

Participating in an Oral History Project

An oral history project gathers and curates oral histories of groups of people united by a specific realm of experience, time period, or heritage. There are oral history projects that focus on jazz musicians, coal miners, former foreign service officers, people who have grown up working along the Chesapeake Bay, armed services veterans, Polish American polka bands—just about anything you can imagine! Some seek to document the lives of the famous—politicians, actors, writers, business leaders, sports figures—while others chronicle the life experiences of everyday folk. Their aim? To preserve important personal histories and find the common threads therein.

To find the oral history project that's the right fit for your interview, do some Internet research. Start with the Oral History Association, the professional organization for oral history practitioners in the U.S.; its website provides links to many oral history centers and collections. Many local historical societies, community organizations, museums, and academic institutions sponsor oral history projects, so those are good places to look as well.

Donating to an Archives

What is an archives? Here's one of the ways the Society of American Archivists defines the term: "An organization that collects the records of individuals, families, or other organizations."

Essentially, an archives preserves documents of enduring value; maintains physical and intellectual control over its holdings; organizes materials so as to preserve essential context; and makes materials accessible to researchers.

Many organizations maintain archives: the government, historical societies, churches, businesses, academic institutions, museums, and libraries, to name a few. Like oral history projects, each archives has a focus. Academic archives often collect materials belonging to individuals of note: scientists, writers, politicians, and artists. Government and business archives focus on materials created by their employees. State historical archives collect materials from local individuals, families, and businesses of note. Still others deal mainly with communities bound by a common history or shared beliefs.

AN ARCHIVAL BOX

Store your interview materials together in an archival box that's just the right size—not so large that the items can tumble around and get damaged, nor so small that documents will crumple or tear when you try to pull them out. For the best protection from dust and environmental contaminants, choose boxes that close completely, not the kind with openings for handles. Label the box with the name of your interview subject.

How did you feel when you first found out you were going to be a parent? Did your reaction surprise you?

A list of archives can be found on the Library of Congress's website for the National Union Catalog of Manuscript Collections. Also check out the "Repositories of Primary Sources" link, where you'll find information on thousands of archival collections worldwide. There are also many unlisted, smaller, local and community organizations that may have an interest in acquiring your recordings. If you feel you've recorded a life history that might be a fit for a particular archives, get in touch.

Creating Your Own Archives

If you're not interested in sending your materials away, you can preserve them safely at home in a personal archives. You'll have to prepare the materials for storage, decide where to store them, and devise a way to "pass them forward" to future caretakers, just as a professional archivist would.

Start by gathering all the documents you'd like to maintain in your archives—the things that you think will be of enduring value to *you*. You'll begin, of course, with your interview materials (though they tell someone else's story, they also belong to you, their cocreator). What else to include? Be on the lookout for the following items:

❖ Diaries

❖ Letters and cards

❖ Photographs

❖ Home movies

DON'T FORGET THE LABEL

What's in that box? Store your interview materials without proper labeling and you might as well toss them into the wind. Unmarked audio or videotapes, CDs, DVDs, or transcripts among miscellaneous documents and papers may represent untold hours of sorting work. Your befuddled heirs won't likely take the time to figure out what those boxes contain—so help them along. Clear labeling is a very important step toward protecting the future of the stories you've collected.

❖ Scrapbooks

❖ Genealogical information

❖ Birth certificates

❖ Marriage licenses

❖ Legal documents such as deeds and naturalization papers

❖ Announcements of major life events such as birth, baptism, and graduation

❖ Awards and commendations

❖ Theater programs and ticket stubs

❖ Travel documents

❖ School and health records

What did your childhood home look like? Can you remember its sights, sounds, smells?

Organize and Sort

Help future family historians navigate your personal archives by establishing a clear organizational system. Each category of documents might require a slightly different treatment. Your interview materials should be clearly labeled with the name of your interviewee. Your collection of letters might be organized chronologically or by correspondent. It makes sense to keep diaries, date books, and calendars in chronological order. If your slides, photos, and home movies are not already organized, decide on a method (chronological, by location, by subject) and stick with it. For a collection of legal documents, consider filing them either by type—for example, wills, birth certificates, deeds—or chronologically.

If you want to go the extra mile, create a "key" to your filing system—a document explaining your organizing systems—and keep it with the archives.

Preparing Your Materials for Storage

Review "Preservation Know-How" (page 130) for tips on best practices for archival materials. Some additional preparation tips:

❖ Provide extra protection to any original paper documents by placing them in protective archival paper or plastic enclosures.

❖ Transparent plastic or Mylar sleeves offer the advantage of allowing you to view documents without handling (and potentially damaging) them. Buy quality materials from reputable vendors of archival supplies for true peace of mind.

❖ Unfold documents for storage; folded papers will eventually weaken at the creases, and may tear when handled.

❖ Store photographs and photographic negatives in appropriately-sized archival enclosures.

Beware of Unfriendly Materials

You'd be surprised at how easily ordinary office supplies can damage documents and photos. Metal fasteners can dig into paper or rust over time, leaving tears or rust stains behind. Before putting documents away, remove any staples and metal paper clips or binder clips; replace with plastic paper clips if necessary. (If the papers are well organized, labeled, and separated into folders, there's really no need for clips at all.) Rubber bands and elastic can become a real mess over time as well; they break down as they age, turning into sticky globs, or drying out and crumbling into grimy dust. If you want to

> ### BUT I HAVE NO ROOM!
>
> For many people, space may be an issue; maintaining a family archives in tight quarters can be a challenge. Try to think outside the box. Does a sibling have a spacious home? Maybe you could partner in maintaining the archives.

bind materials together, use ribbonlike cotton tape, available from archival supply vendors. What about regular cellophane adhesive tape? Don't even think about it! If a document is torn, place it in a clear plastic enclosure rather than trying to "repair" it with adhesive tape (which in time can stain the paper and may be difficult to remove without damaging the document); or reinforce it with archival-quality "document repair" tape.

A Healthy Storage Environment

The environment in which you store your materials could well determine how long they'll survive. Institutional archives often maintain their historical records in rooms kept at temperature and humidity levels that are specific to the medium stored there— paper, photographic stock, film, magnetic tape. That's impractical at home, but temperature and humidity are the two main factors to consider when deciding where to store your materials.

Again, don't store your materials in places where you would not be comfortable. You wouldn't thrive in an ovenlike attic, damp crawl space, or musty basement, and neither will recordings, papers, and photographs. Additional considerations? Keep the materials out of direct sunlight and protected from dust and any potential pollutants. Garages and outdoor storage sheds are especially unsuitable because they're not weatherproof or climate controlled, and also because anything stored there is susceptible to mold, dust, potentially destructive fumes, and visits from voracious critters such as squirrels, mice, rats, and insects. And don't forget the possibility of water damage from indoor floods and leaks: Store your collection off the floor and as far as possible from windows, water pipes, and plumbing fixtures. (That includes overhead risks too—bathrooms, kitchens, or laundry rooms on higher floors.)

A fireproof safe or file cabinet is an ideal storage space—but any well-chosen spot will offer a degree of protection.

Expanding Your Archives

Once you've got the archival bug, you may find your interests spiraling out from there. You may want to go on and create a bona fide *family*

THE FUTURE OF YOUR ARCHIVES

As you plan for the future custody of your personal archives—which includes your interview materials—it's a good idea to leave written instructions naming the next custodian for the documents. For a family archives, you'll need to have participating individuals sign deed of gift agreements that give permission for the ongoing use of their contributions. On an additional, separate sheet for each person, list the agreed upon *intended* uses for the materials and include *any restrictions* concerning access that may need to be monitored. File this information and the signed agreement with the rest of the contributor's materials.

archives. Consider all the documents a family creates, collects, and saves over time . . . they fill desks, drawers, file cabinets, attics.

Those caches can be treasure troves. In their attic, one family found a stash of documents in an old saxophone case—right where the clan's patriarch, a World War II veteran, had left it years before. There were his service medals and discharge papers, tiny black-and-white snapshots of his army buddies in the South Pacific, a sheaf of lively letters from a hometown friend serving in Italy, a "Dear John" letter he'd received toward the end of the war, Christmas cards from grade school classmates, a condolence card from his high school teacher upon the death of his beloved mother, a diary he began a year later. The children saw a whole new side of the father they'd always known as tight-lipped and stoic.

Not every family will be so lucky, though—usually, an individual needs to take the lead in working to preserve a family's heritage.

Get Your Family Involved

Encourage family members to take an interest in preserving and using the documents in the archives; the more a family archives is *used*, the more likely it is to be valued and lovingly passed along. Try some of these tactics for sharing its contents:

❖ Start by asking family members to contribute. Grandparents may be happy to unload boxes of old photos and home movies. Children can add their birth announcements, school photos, artwork, and report cards.

❖ Take the time to get together and listen to those family stories you recorded.

❖ Periodically review the collection together, perhaps during the holidays or at birthday celebrations.

❖ Give school-age children copies (never originals!) of some of your older documents for use in school projects. Old diaries and letters can form the basis of writing assignments or art projects—and, of course, they make fascinating reading in and of themselves.

❖ Explore online archives and genealogy resources with your family to see if you can find old documents relating to your relatives or ancestors, such as ships' manifests (passenger lists) for those who immigrated to the United States. Add such findings to your archives.

❖ Take children along to historical societies, libraries, or archives when you do research and have them participate.

❖ Turn archiving into detective work to pique children's interest. Offer a challenge: *Let's figure out the identities of the people in this old photograph. This little girl looks like your mother. What year could the photo have been taken, and where?*

❖ Take photos of unidentified people or places along to family reunions and see if anyone can provide information.

❖ Create a family website on which children can post some of their documents; use secure settings and a password to ensure that family privacy remains intact.

When You Lose Someone . . .

When we lose a loved one, we often rush blindly through the task of sorting through and clearing out personal documents. Stunned, and in a hurry to accomplish a painful chore, we may toss and give away what we really should keep.

The best thing to do in the moment is to store as much of the materials as possible, even if they are a confusing mess. Postpone decisions until you can find time to examine the documents.

A Final Word . . .

When you're ready to distribute your recordings, transcripts, scrapbooks, or writing, don't forget to include a note or letter to the recipients. Describe your role in the interview process and include your thoughts about the gift—and be sure to explain any limitations on its use. If the interviewee has requested that access to his words be limited, provide the names of those who *are* permitted access.

Make It a Series

Emboldened by your first oral history project? Why not do a series of related interviews—your subject's siblings, spouse, friends, or neighbors? It may be an ambitious task, but it's a valuable one. Woven together, the stories will create a larger picture of a time, place, and community. They'll also add immeasurably to the portrait of your first subject: As friends or family members tell their versions of the same story, a fuller and more complex account will emerge. And the cycle of stories continues on.

A Wonderful Gift

Everyone involved in the interview process—you, your interviewee, and those who hear or read the interview or enjoy the projects it inspired—will find pleasure in and gain insights from your work. Because you made the effort and took the time to honor your interviewee, because you made sure his life story was recorded; because you chose to give back some of the love you've received and to show your respect—history now includes this person. His story will live on in new generations—*because of you.*

How did the relationship with your partner evolve over the years? What got better and what got worse?

Appendix

Forms & Resources

To reproduce the forms on the following pages, increase the page size to 122 percent on a photocopier. Sample legal forms courtesy of the Oral History Association. Copyright © 1985, 1993, 2002 by the Oral History Association. All rights reserved. These forms and provisions are presented for informational purposes only. They do not attempt to reflect the law as it may apply to such releases on either the federal level or in each of the fifty states, and they may not provide the legal protection you want or need in your particular situation.

Life History Worksheet

Interviewee name: _____

Current address: _____

Phone number: _____

E-mail: _____

Interviewer name: _____

Current address: _____

Phone number: _____

E-mail: _____

Interview location: _____

Interview date: _____

Interviewee's place and date of birth: _____

Residences (with approximate dates):

_____   _____

_____   _____

_____   _____

_____   _____

_____   _____

Educational history: _____

_____

_____

_____

_____

Job history (dates and brief descriptions):

_____   _____

_____   _____

_____   _____

_____   _____

_____   _____

Memberships and associations (unions, clubs, churches, synagogues, etc.):

_____

_____

_____

_____

_____

FATHER: (name) _____
(place and date of birth) _____
(occupation) _____

MOTHER: (name) _____
(place and date of birth) _____
(occupation) _____

SIBLINGS: (name/place and date of birth)

_____   _____
_____   _____
_____   _____
_____   _____
_____   _____

CHILDREN: (name/place and date of birth)

_____   _____
_____   _____
_____   _____
_____   _____
_____   _____

GRANDPARENTS: (name/place and date of birth)

_____   _____
_____   _____
_____   _____
_____   _____

OTHER FAMILY MEMBERS AND FRIENDS: (name/place and date of birth)

_____   _____
_____   _____
_____   _____
_____   _____
_____   _____
_____   _____
_____   _____
_____   _____
_____   _____
_____   _____
_____   _____
_____   _____

Field Notes

Interviewee name: _____

Interview date and time: _____

Interview location: _____

Interviewer name: _____

General impressions of interview: _____
_____
_____
_____

General mood and energy level of interviewee: _____
_____
_____
_____

Description of interview environment (What, if anything, did the environment add to the portrait of the interviewee?): _____
_____
_____
_____

Ways in which the recording environment enhanced or impeded the exchange of questions and answers: _____
_____
_____
_____

Conversation made prior to and after the recording: _____
_____
_____
_____

Interruptions—cause, length, and resolution: _____
_____
_____
_____

"Off-the-record" discussions, triggers, and topics: _____
_____
_____
_____

Additional persons at the interview: _____
_____
_____

Usage Agreement

In consideration for the audio or video recording, editing, and preservation of my oral history interview (or oral memoir) by _____
(*name of individual, archive, or program*) consisting of _____
_____ (*description of materials*), I, _____
(*name of interviewee*), of _____ (*address*),
_____ (*city*), _____ (*state and*
zip code), herein relinquish and transfer to _____
(*individual, archive, or program*) my interview (or oral memoir) so that it may be made available to researchers and others and may be quoted from, published or broadcast in any medium or form that _____ (*individual, archive,* *or program*) deems appropriate.

In making this contract I understand that I am conveying to _____
_____ (*individual, archive, or program*) all legal title and literary property rights which I have or may be deemed to have in my interview (or oral memoir) as well as my right, title and interest in any copyright, which may be secured under the laws now or later in force and effect in the United States of America. My conveyance of copyright encompasses the exclusive rights of: reproduction, distribution, preparation of derivative works, public performance, public display as well as all renewals and extensions.

_____ Date _____
Signature of Interviewee

_____ Date _____
Signature of Interviewer or Agent/Representative of archives or program

Deed of Gift

I, _____ (*name of interviewee*), of
_____ (*address*), _____ (*city*),
_____ (*state and zip code*), herein permanently give,
convey, and assign to _____ (*name of individual, archive
or program*), which is currently in possession of my interview (or oral memoir) consisting
of _____ (*description of materials*).

In so doing I understand that my interview (or oral memoir) will be made available to
researchers and others and may be quoted from, published or broadcast in any medium
that _____ (*individual, archive, or program*)
shall deem appropriate.

In making this gift I fully understand that I am conveying all legal title and literary property rights which I have or may be deemed to have in my interview (or oral memoir)
as well as all rights, title, and interest in any copyright which may be secured under the
laws now or later in force and effect in the United States of America. My conveyance
of copyright encompasses the exclusive rights of: reproduction, distribution, preparation of derivative works, public performance, public display as well as all renewals and
extensions.

I, _____ (*agent for or the duly appointed
representative of*) _____ (*name of individual, archives, or
program*) accept the interview (or oral memoir) of _____
(*name of interviewee*) for inclusion into the _____
(*name of archive or program*).

_____ Date _____
Signature of Interviewee

_____ Date _____
Signature of Interviewer

_____ Date _____

Public Domain Declaration

In making this gift I fully understand that my interview or oral memoir will not be copyrighted by me _____ (*name of interviewee*) or by _____ (*name of interviewer*) but is to be placed in the public domain. This action is intended to facilitate usage by future researchers.

_____ Date _____
Signature of Interviewee

_____ Date _____
Signature of Interviewer

If the interviewee wants to make a gift of the interview materials to an individual, archives, or program and to simultaneously make a *Public Domain Declaration,* alter the *Deed of Gift* form (on facing page) by replacing the paragraph beginning with the phrase "In making this gift" with the following: "In making this gift I fully understand that my interview or oral memoir will not be copyrighted by me or by _____ (*name of individual, archive or program*), but is to be placed in the public domain. This action is intended to facilitate usage by future researchers."

Books and Articles for Further Reading

Baum, Willa K. *Transcribing and Editing Oral History.* Nashville: American Association for State and Local History, 1977.

Clark, Roy Peter. *Writing Tools: 50 Essential Strategies for Every Writer.* New York: Little, Brown and Company, 2006.

Crystal, Billy. *700 Sundays.* New York: Warner Books, 2005.

Gross, Terry. *All I Did Was Ask.* New York: Hyperion, 2004.

Guide To Donating Your Personal or Family Papers to a Repository. Manuscript Repositories Section of the Society of American Archivists. Available online at www.archivists.org/publications/donating-familyrecs.asp.

Hart, Cynthia. *Cynthia Hart's Scrapbook Workshop.* New York: Workman Publishing, 1998.

Neuenschwander, John A. *Oral History and the Law.* Edited by Mary Kay Quinlan. Oral History Association, 2002.

The Oral History Reader, Second Edition. Edited by Robert Perks and Alistair Thomson. New York: Routledge, 2006.

Principles and Standards of the Oral History Association. Oral History Association. Available online at www.oralhistory.org/do-oral-history/oral-history-evaluation-guidelines/#1.3.

Remen, Rachel Naomi, M.D. *Kitchen Table Wisdom, Stories That Heal.* New York: Riverhead Books, 1996.

Ritchie, Donald A. *Doing Oral History.* New York: Oxford University Press, 2003.

Ritzenthaler, Mary Lynn. *Preserving Archives and Manuscripts.* Chicago: Society of American Archivists, 1993.

Thompson, Paul. *The Voice of the Past: Oral History.* New York: Oxford University Press, 2000.

Oral History on the Web

The Oral History Association (www.oralhistory.org/) is the national professional organization for oral history practitioners in the United States. Its website includes links to oral history centers and collections and information on new technology. It publishes a pamphlet series on conducting various kinds of oral history projects—family, classroom, and community.

The oldest and largest organized oral history program in the world, Columbia University's Oral History Research Office (www.columbia.edu/cu/lweb/indiv/oral/about.html) provides online access to many projects.

George Mason University's "History Matters: The U.S. Survey Course on the Web" includes an insightful essay, "Making Sense of Oral History" (http://historymatters.gmu.edu/mse/oral/), by Linda Shopes, past president of the Oral History Association.

The Library of Congress's American Folklife Center (www.loc.gov/folklife/) has vast collections of audio and video recordings, folklore, interviews, and oral histories. Two extraordinary ongoing projects are the Veterans History Project at www.loc.gov/vets/ and StoryCorps at www.loc.gov/folklife/storycorpsfaq.html. StoryCorps also maintains its own website (www.storycorps.org/).

The Library of Congress's American Memory project (http://memory.loc.gov/ammen/collections) makes the materials in some historical collections available online.

The website for the Louie B. Nunn Center for Oral History at the University of Kentucky (www.uky.edu/Libraries/libpage.php?lweb_id=11&llib_id=13) includes good technical information about recording.

Archives and Preservation Information on the Web

ArchiveGrid (http://archivegrid.org/) is a great resource for finding "historical documents, personal papers, and family histories held in archives around the world." It's available only through libraries that are members of the Online Computer Library Center (OCLC) (www.oclc.org).

The Association of Motion Image Archivists (AMIA) (www.amianet.org/) is a professional organization "established to advance the field of moving image archiving …." It provides a variety of links to other extraordinary websites concerned with issues relating to film and video.

The Association for Recorded Sound Collections (ARSC) (www.arsc-audio.org/) is dedicated to "the preservation and study of sound recordings."

The directory of Archival Organizations in the United States and Canada (www.archivists.org/assoc-orgs/directory/index.asp) provides contact information for nearly 70 national, regional, state, provincial, and local professional archival associations.

Home Movie Day (www.homemovieday.com) is an annual worldwide event, started by archivists in 2002, that celebrates the rich cultural universe captured by amateur filmmakers in home movies. People with old home movies—whether their own, or inherited from family and friends—are encouraged to bring them to selected locations on Home Movie Day, where archivists will evaluate their condition and discuss preservation issues that they pose. If the movies are in good enough shape they are screened. This celebration is a project of the Center for Home Movies.

According to its mission statement, the Image Permanence Institute (http://imagepermanenceinstitute.org) is a "recognized world leader in the development and deployment of sustainable practices for the preservation of images and cultural property." For up-to-date information on preservation, this is the site to use.

The National Film Preservation Organization (www.filmpreservation.org/) is a nonprofit organization created by the U.S. Congress to help save America's film heritage.

The website of the Northeast Document Conservation Center (www.nedcc.org/) provides a tremendous amount of preservation information. Their webpage "Resources for Private and Family Collections" (www.nedcc.org/resources/resources.php) provides detailed advice on protecting your family documents.

The "Repositories of Primary Sources" website (www.uidaho.edu/special-collections/Other.Repositories.html) provides links to thousands of archives and other primary sources; though it's intended mainly for researchers, it may prove helpful in identifying a home for your interview materials.

The Society of American Archivists (SAA) (http://archivists.org) is the oldest and largest national archival professional organization in North America.

Transom.org describes itself as "an experiment in channeling new work and voices to public radio through the Internet, and for discussing that work, and encouraging more." Along the way the organization has developed a variety of useful tools to help in recording audio, and conducting interviews. Especially interesting for anyone thinking of working with children is *Shout Out: A Kid's Guide to Recording Stories,* by Katie Davis with the Urban Rangers (http://transom.org/tools/basics/200501.shoutout.kdavis.html).

WorldCat (www.worldcat.org/) is useful for searching libraries worldwide to find materials of interest, including archival collections.

Archival Supplies

Note: *These purveyors are devoted to archival supplies, but scrapbooking stores, stationery stores, and other paper-goods retailers may also be good sources.*

Archival Methods (www.archivalmethods.com/), 235 Middle Road, Henrietta, NY 14467. Phone: 866-877-7050. Fax: 585-334-7067. E-mail: mail@archivalmethods.com.

Archivart® Products for Conservation and Restoration (www.archivart.com), 40 Eisenhower Drive, Paramus, NJ 07652. Phone: 800-804-8428. Fax: 888-273-4824. E-mail: askarchivart@nbframing.com.

Brodart (www.shopbrodart.com), P.O. Box 300, McElhattan, PA, 17748. Phone: 888-820-4377. Fax: 800-283-6087. E-mail: supplies.customerservice@brodart.com.

Gaylord Bros (www.gaylordmart.com), P.O. Box 4901, Syracuse, NY 13221. Phone: 800-962-9580. Fax: 800-272-3412. If ordering in Canada: 800-841-5854. Fax: 800-615-3779.

Hollinger Corporation (www.genealogicalstorageproducts.com), Phone: 800-634-0491. Fax: 800-947-8814. E-mail: hollingercorp@earthlink.net.

Light Impressions (www.lightimpressionsdirect.com), P.O. Box 2100, Santa Fe Springs, CA 90670. Phone: 800-828-6216. Fax: 800-828-5539. E-mail: info@lightimpressionsdirect.com.

Metal Edge (www.metaledgeinc.com/), 6340 Bandini Avenue, Commerce, CA 90040. Phone: 800-862-2228. Fax: 888-822-6937. E-mail: info@metaledgeinc.com.

Talas (www.talas-nyc.com/), 330 Morgan Avenue, Brooklyn, NY 11211. Phone: 212-219-0770. Fax: 212-219-0735. E-mail: info@talasonline.com.

University Products (www.archival suppliers.com/), 517 Main Street, Holyoke, MA 01040. Phone: 800-628-1912. Fax: 413-532-9281. E-mail: info@universityproducts.com, custserv@universityproducts.com.

In the U.K.: Preservation Equipment Ltd. (www.preservationequipment.com/Home), Vinces Road, Diss, Norfolk IP22 4HQ, England. Phone: 44 (0)1379 647400. Fax: 44 (0) 1379 650582. E-mail: info@preservationequipment.com.

Audio/Video Transfers and Duplication

Note: *This short list of organizations dedicated to the preservation of audio and video materials might be a good starting point for information on transferring or duplicating your audio or videotapes, but you should also be able to find vendors on the Web or in the phone book.*

The Association for Recorded Sound Collections, ARSC (www.arsc-audio .org/), provides links to a directory of members who offer audio preservation and restoration services at www.arsc-audio.org/pdf/Directory2009-02.pdf.

Home Movie Day's website provides information on film labs that transfer small gauge films (www.homemovieday .com/transfer.html), some of which also transfer various video formats.

A list of UK film labs that specialize in film and video transfers can be found at www.nationalmediamuseum.org .uk/pdfs/FI%20LM_AND_VIDEO_TRANSFER_SERVICES.pdf.

Vermont Folklife Center's Field Research guides (www.vermontfolklifecenter.org/archive/archive-fieldguides.html) include the following: Digital Audio Field Recording Equipment Guide, Audio Recording Equipment Guide: Retired Equipment List, Field Recording in the Digital Age, Digital Editing of Field Audio, Resources on the Preservation of Materials in Ethnographic and Oral History Collections.

Editing and Transcription Guidance

Vermont Folklife Center has an excellent guide to editing, "Digital Editing of Field Audio" (www.vermontfolklifecenter.org/archive/res_digitalediting.htm).

Transom.org has a terrific column focused on editing audio (http://transom.org/tools/editing_mixing/) and a discussion page, "Tools Talk," where you can post questions.

Transcription information is available from the *Veterans History Project*: www.loc .gov/vets/transcribe.html.

At *Videomaker* magazine's website (www.videomaker.com/learn/) you'll find useful information on video editing and production.

Acknowledgments

For her creativity, determination, and generous contributions, I thank Lisa Samson.

For guiding us ever onward, I thank our editor, Savannah Ashour. For their heartfelt determination to make this book the best it could be, I thank Peter Workman, Susan Bolotin, and Janet Vicario. For their work on the book's cover and interior design, I thank David Matt, Julie Duquet, Robb Allen, and Janet Parker. For his commitment to production excellence, I thank Doug Wolff. And for their important contributions, I thank Janet Harris, Carol White, Randall Lotowycz, Nathan Lifton, and the rest of the editorial, sales, publicity, and marketing staff at Workman Publishing.

For creating, providing, and appearing in the snapshots published in this book, I thank all the known and now-unknown photographers and subjects as well as the antiques dealers who helped preserve the vintage images and made them available to me.

For his unfailingly astute comments and for being an inspiration, I thank my son, Thomas Ando-Hart.

For their steadfast support and gracious help, I thank Bonnie Slotnick, Larry Price, Sharyn Prentiss, Gayle Hart, Imogene Smith, Barbara Salisbury, Howard Berg, Ron Stegall, Mari and Jason Tuttle, Pat Upton, and Janet Saghatelian.

For granting permission to use their legal forms, I thank Madelyn Campbell and the Oral History Association.

Many people contributed in various ways at different stages in the creation of this book. Please know that whether or not your contribution is noted here, every smidgen of help you provided is, was, and will always be deeply appreciated.
——*Cynthia Hart*

For her enormous well of creative energy and her boundless determination to produce a book that is both useful and beautiful, I thank Cynthia Hart.

For first introducing me to the power and pleasure of storytelling, I thank my father, Lyle, and for her inspiring determination to record stories of underdocumented women, I thank my mother, Lois. I thank my sisters, Cindi and Sara, and my brothers, Kurt, Karl, and Eric, for sharing wild times and hysterical stories with me over the years. I am especially grateful to Cindi for her insightful review of early drafts and for the grace and humor with which she continually guides me, and to Sara for her steadying words of encouragement.

I thank my extended family—the Walsh, Samson, Betz, Shah, Palmer, and Jatkowski clans—and all the friends who have shared stories of their life adventures with me. Having such wonderful folk to bounce ideas off of has been both invaluable and great fun.

For generously sharing their knowledge of archives and public history, I thank Peter Wosh, Rachel Bernstein, and the rest of the faculty in the History Department at NYU. For encouraging my first steps working in archives, I thank Joseph Komljenovich and Andy Lanset. And I thank the staff at Swarthmore College's Friends Historical Library, especially Pat O'Donnell, for the warmth and support they have offered me.

The love of my life, Edwin Betz, centers and inspires me, and our sons, Arnav Shah and Jonathan Betz, give me great joy. I appreciate the encouragement— and challenges—I receive from them daily.

—*Lisa Samson*